Adventure in Human Knowledges and Beliefs

Andrew Ralls Woodward

Hamilton Books

A member of
Rowman & Littlefield
Lanham • Boulder • New York • Toronto • Plymouth, UK

Copyright © 2014 by Hamilton Books
4501 Forbes Boulevard, Suite 200, Lanham, Maryland 20706
Hamilton Books Aquisitions Department (301) 459-3366

10 Thornbury Road, Plymouth PL6 7PP, United Kingdom

All rights reserved

British Library Cataloguing in Publication Information Available

Library of Congress Control Number: 2014940663
ISBN: 978-0-7618-6408-0

To

My friends of all ages,

who I met in my early 20s,

in Canada, Switzerland, and Israel

"We might call ourselves atheist, theist or agnostic. However, in the grand scheme of things, we all share one thing: we share human knowledges and beliefs."

A. Woodward,

Leader of *Adventure in Human Knowledges and Beliefs*

Contents

Prologue: *This Book* and Acknowledgments	vii
I: Knowledge or Knowledges? Belief or Beliefs?	**1**
1 The Adventure	3
2 Knowledges	5
3 Beliefs	15
4 Belief as Trust	25
II: Scientific and Religious People	**31**
5 Religious Language	33
6 Some Unexpected Surprises	37
7 Faces of Religion / Faces of Science	45
8 Knowledge and Belief Communities	53
III: Adjudicators	**61**
9 Causes and Explanatory Forces	63
10 The "Knowledge Bar"	73
11 Ancient Forms of Knowledge	81
12 The Current Landscape	87
Epilogue: What Then Is *Reality*?	91
Glossary of Strange Sounding Words	93
Bibliography of Works Cited	95

Index 97

Prologue: *This Book* and Acknowledgments

This book isn't meant to be a complicated book, but rather a concise and useful book. If learning isn't useful it doesn't really have a purpose. The idea for this book came while I was doing the coursework in my doctorate at the University of Toronto. I was thinking about my dissertation project which involves the philosophy of science as a model for religious knowledge. I read many different books—popular and academic—on the relationship between science and religion. None of the books really dealt with the philosophical questions of knowledge and belief in a way that was accessible to a wide audience of readers. Sure, the academic books covered epistemology (the *form of knowledge*) but those books were not meant for a wide audience, and the popular books were just missing some really important philosophical content. My hope is that this book will help to fill a gap in this area, providing an opportunity for everyone to learn about the mysteries of human knowledges and beliefs. I have, of course, relied on the scholarly works of 20th and 21st century authors as my sources, and you will find references to those people throughout. Part of my aim was to capture the pivotal themes of their works, so that after you finish reading this book you will have a good sense of the philosophical landscape of science and religion.

My professors in Toronto have been the greatest academic mentors and my confidence as a student grew steadily under their watch. Thank you to Professor Donald Wiebe who read my manuscript and who gave me advice and encouragement along the way. Thanks to Trinity College in the University of Toronto, where as a Junior Fellow I had the freedom to transition from engineering and theological studies toward a doctorate in the philosophy of science and religion. Thank you to my mom and dad, my brother, and my Woodward aunts and uncles, who were always there for a phone call or email while I completed my degrees and who supported me in various ways as I made the academic jump from engineering to the liberal arts.

Finally I am greatly indebted to the "knowledge and belief" experiences I had in my early 20s and to the people who helped to shape those experiences. My undergraduate degree in engineering chemistry provided me with exposure to the lives of scientific and engineering people. My work as a school chaplain in a high school and my work as a preacher in a small town church gave me exposure to the lives of people who were interested in having a faith. A university course I took in Tel Aviv gave me some familiarity with the Middle East. The middle school students, who stayed at a school in Switzerland where I worked, asked me some very tough but intriguing questions about belief. I worked in Toronto as a teaching assistant for a university course on science and religion and taught some lectures about a possible compatibility system between knowledge and belief communities. Most of the practical experience I bring to this book arose from these events. I would like all of you who were with me at those places (you know who you are!) to understand that you all had important roles to play as I wrote this book—you all taught me something and for that I am grateful.

I

Knowledge or Knowledges?
Belief or Beliefs?

Chapter One

The Adventure

Knowledges and beliefs have existed since the time our human species *Homo sapiens* first walked the earth. Although we may think we already know what knowledges or beliefs are, to get to the heart of our adventure we really must go back to the beginning—back to what is happening at the core of *claiming* knowledges and beliefs. I invite you to participate in this adventure—you, I, and all the readers of this book. There are only two conditions. These conditions are necessary for us to fully enjoy the experience of this adventure and to learn and grow along the way. The conditions are as follows:

1. We must be willing to let go of whatever rigidness prevents us from taking a *neutral, dispassionate,* and *unbiased* look at our own world views whether they be a science or a religion. I mean that. Make a conscious effort right now to drop whatever it is that keeps you from re-adjusting or re-evaluating your own knowledges and beliefs. I am not asking you to discard whatever you think (in the end, you probably won't need to) but we do need to be *open* to considering alternative world views. A *world view* is the "lens" through which you see the world—your own personal opinion on any issue, the language you speak, the job you have, or the things you do for fun on the weekend. Any of these factors might contribute to your world view. Your world view also includes your knowledges and beliefs.
2. We must be willing to become adjudicators. You will be your own adjudicator, I will be my own adjudicator, and everyone else reading this book will be their own adjudicators. An *adjudicator* is a person who has to choose a single option from many options. Other descriptions for *adjudicator* might be *judge* or *decision maker*. The best analogy for an adjudicator that I can think of is when we go grocery

shopping. We've all done this. We stand in an aisle—let's say the pasta aisle as an example—and we look at all the various types of spaghetti sauce that are available for us to choose from. Generally, we end up choosing only one type of sauce, because that is all that we need, but, in the process of thinking about which type of sauce to choose, we were acting as adjudicators (or judges or decision makers). This book is about being a special kind of adjudicator (nothing to do with spaghetti, of course!) who judges the acceptability of knowledges and beliefs. I'll let you discover for yourself the exact role of being this kind of adjudicator and what all of this means as we journey through our adventure.

If you are unsure of what I mean by any of the words mentioned above, that is fine, because I will explain all and all will become clear. In fact, as the leader of this adventure, I consider it my own responsibility to make sure that no one is left trailing behind. (There was a time when I did not know what all of these words meant either.) For now, the two conditions I have just mentioned can really be put more simply as: i) While reading this book, keep an open mind, and ii) Don't be afraid to trust your own instincts. Also, as we move along, I will do my best to explain any strange sounding words as they come up. However, in the event that you require an explanation before I get to providing one in the text, you will find at the end a glossary, which provides a concise explanation for each strange sounding word in this book. I think the glossary should help alleviate any potential complications for vocabulary.

This adventure is very exciting, because we are bridging what some would say is unbridgeable—we are going to translate some unusual ideas into ideas that all of us will appreciate and understand (regardless of our own career backgrounds). We are going to learn some very interesting things that don't usually get covered in a book that is meant for a wide audience. Also, keep in mind that you don't have to necessarily like everything in this book (if you like it all, that's great), but you can still learn something useful even if you don't like it or don't agree with it. It is okay, too, if you decide to read a single page more than once. Take as much time as you need to understand each chapter. You might like to read a single chapter each night in between the other books you are currently reading, or you might like to read this entire book during a single day over the weekend. (There are many possibilities for how you can participate in this adventure.) Now, with all of that introduction aside, let us begin our adventure. . . .

Chapter Two

Knowledges

There is a tendency in our 21st century Western life to speak of one type of knowledge, or to simply say, "knowledge." Usually the term *knowledge* is used to characterize the products or content of the natural science and engineering disciplines. Indeed, this is the situation in modern universities where these subjects are taught and studied. The term *belief* on the other hand is generally used to characterize the products or content of religions. This, too, tends to be the situation in modern universities where religious studies or theology departments exist. Moreover we find this scientific and religious distinction between the terms *knowledge* and *belief* being used in the philosophy departments of universities. There are good reasons for all of this to be the case. Let me leave aside belief for a moment, and focus on knowledge. If you are a pro-belief (religious) person, do not lose heart, because I will suggest later that religion can be a type of knowledge (although a very different type of knowledge from scientific knowledge). When we speak about scientific knowledge we are talking about a type of theory-generating or fact-gathering activity about natural states of affairs in the world. The techniques that we use to gather facts and test theories about states of affairs in the world are completed through various types of scientific investigations and engineering designs. I will not delve very much into the various types of scientific or engineering disciplines, because that is not the purpose of our adventure. Rather, I will point out a special trait that all scientific and engineering knowledge possesses. A trait that, as we shall see, is perhaps not so present in religious knowledge. (There, you see, I have now used the word *knowledge* along with the word *religious*.) The trait that makes science such an attractive and useful type of knowledge is that it is a type of knowledge that is *open to change*. It is a type of knowledge that can be corrected through experience and this is what makes learning possible. This is the reason why universities have chosen to adopt *scientific knowledge* as their benchmark for teaching and research in many disciplines. But, what exactly does it mean for scientific knowledge to be *open to change*?

It is difficult to define the term *science* so that everyone will agree with the definition. The etymology of the word *science* is the Latin word *scientia*, a noun, meaning *knowledge*. With this in mind, a definition for science is that science is knowledge about the natural world. However, science is really much more than this. Science is special because science has the ability to always improve itself. Even Sir Isaac Newton (b. 1642, d. 1727), who was the greatest scientist of his time, possessed less scientific knowledge than a high school student of science possesses today. About himself, Newton is thought to have said, "I do not know what I may appear to the world, but to myself I seem to have been only like a boy playing on the seashore . . . whilst [while] the great ocean of truth lay all undiscovered before me."[1] Newton was well aware that, in the future, science would improve.

We apply the term *scientist* to many people throughout history (such as Newton), because many people did scientific work. However, the term *scientist* is only about 170 years old. It was William Whewell, the Master of Trinity College in the University of Cambridge, who popularized the term *scientist* sometime around 1840. Prior to that time, people who did scientific work were often called natural philosophers. Take a step outside of science and we have engineering, an activity which uses scientific knowledge to design and create products to benefit human beings and the world in which they live. The term *engineering* is derived from the Latin word *ingenium*, meaning *talent*. Quite often we find scientists working on the growth of scientific knowledge—understanding current knowledge and figuring out new knowledge. We find engineers working on designs for products which utilize scientific knowledge. For example, a chemical engineer might design a pharmaceutical product, which benefits human beings by alleviating the effects of an illness. However, before it was possible to design that product, a chemist had to figure out the right combination of chemical molecules that will target and destroy the bacteria cells causing the illness (the scientific knowledge). Some people work as both scientists and engineers. In those cases, a distinction between the activities of science and engineering is not so important.

Thomas S. Kuhn (b. 1922, d. 1996) was a professor of the philosophy and history of science at the Massachusetts Institute of Technology. In Thomas Kuhn's controversial book *The Structure of Scientific Revolutions* (first published 1962) he outlines an epistemology (an explanation coming up soon) for constructing the *form* of scientific knowledge. Kuhn's work will serve as the basis for our adventure of knowledge claims in science. I have chosen to use Kuhn's work, because until he wrote *The Structure of Scientific Revolutions* it was very difficult to analyze science in a neutral, dispassionate, and unbiased way. (To become adjudicators we need to be *neutral, dispassionate, and unbiased* people.) We have just seen a new word *epistemology* [ih-pis-tuh-mol-uh-jee] and a new phrase *knowledge claims*. The word *epistemology* has its origin in the ancient Greek word *episteme*—ἐπιστήμη—which, like *scientia*, also means *knowledge* (go figure). The word *epistemology* was first used by the Scottish philosopher James Frederick Ferrier (b. 1808, d. 1864). Broadly speaking epistemology is a branch of philosophy and theology that asks questions about knowledge claims: What kinds of knowledge claims are legitimate and what kinds are not? How do we adjudicate the acceptability of a knowledge claim? Epistemology is relevant to both science and religion, because both scientific exercises and religious exercises involve making *knowledge claims* about states of affairs in the world. There is our new phrase *knowledge claims* again and we are going to see it throughout the rest of our adventure. A knowledge claim is pretty much what it sounds like. It is a statement of knowledge—scientific or religious—that you or I make. A knowledge claim in science might be the statement: *I claim that an atom is the smallest piece of a chemical element; atoms contain even smaller pieces of matter called electrons and protons*. A knowledge claim in religion might be the statement: *I claim that a superhuman power exists; this power has been around for longer than the world has been around.*

Knowledge claims are connected to our roles as adjudicators. Whenever we make a knowledge claim we are acting as adjudicators whether we realize it, or not. We are asking: what knowledge is legitimate knowledge—what knowledge is *right* knowledge? If we make a knowledge claim, such as the examples of scientific and religious knowledge claims provided in the preceding paragraph, we are probably confident that the statement of knowledge we are claiming is legitimate knowledge. With this in mind, our roles as adjudicators come with a great responsibility—we are the people who have the task of deciding what will count as legitimate (right) knowledge and what will *not* count as legitimate knowledge. It is not just a great responsibility—it is a great *moral* responsibility. More on this later. We are still getting things "set up" so to speak. Think of this chapter as the beginning of the trail. As mentioned, our pertinent question right now is—what exactly does it mean for scientific knowledge to be *open to change*?

In *The Structure of Scientific Revolutions* Thomas Kuhn describes "normal science"[2] as new scientific research that is based on past achievements, especially past achievements that have been acknowledged by a scientific community as being a good foundation for future research. Kuhn was well-known for his use of the term *paradigm* which he described as being closely related to "normal science." He used the concept of paradigms to explain his interpretation of scientific thinking. In general terms a *paradigm* is a pattern or model, similar to the notion of patterns in grammar which allow us to conjugate a verb using a series of pre-established verb endings specific to a particular tense and applied to any verb in a particular model.[3] In the philosophy of science, Kuhn explains that a paradigm is an achievement in science that provides a foundation for future scientific research. Unlike just any achievement in science, a paradigm possesses two qualities: i) the achievement had never been accomplished before,[4] and ii) the achievement left space for new research.[5] Students of science and engineering are familiar with examples of paradigms, even if they do not describe these examples as such. Some examples of paradigms are as follows: molecular orbital diagrams in chemistry, Quantum mechanics in physics, and survival of the fittest through natural selection in biology. In the modern West, it is the study of a paradigm that prepares a science or engineering student to join a particular scientific or engineering community (usually science or engineering students will learn a few different paradigms during their time in university or college). Thomas Kuhn goes on further to tell us that paradigms allow scientists and engineers to resolve disagreements over the foundations of their work and also share rules and structures that will resolve ambiguities, helping them to find a common ground in their practice.[6] Indeed, finding a common ground in scientific work is often very difficult. This is, in part, due to the misunderstanding that science provides us with knowledge of absolute truths. In real life, science does not provide us with knowledge of absolute truths, but science provides us with *theoretical* knowledge about states of affairs in the world. Theoretical knowledge is expressed in the form of scientific theories. Examples of scientific theories are atomic theory, formulated by the chemist John Dalton in the early 1800s, and the general theory of relativity, formulated by the physicist Albert Einstein in 1916.

Over the years, we have understood the nature of scientific theories in various ways. Yes, most of us acknowledge that a scientific theory is not the "truth," but, beyond that, various interpretations have been made as to exactly what a theory is. For some people, called *classical realists*, a theory provides a description of physical reality as reality is. This particular view of a theory is probably the closest view to saying that a theory is the truth. However, it still isn't quite the same thing, because in this view the theory provides a *description* of physical reality, which is different from saying that the theory is the truth. Other people, called *critical realists*, are similar to classical realists, but they are not quite so prepared to say that a theory provides a description of reality as reality is. Rather *critical realists* would prefer to say there is a real "something" to be studied and a theory can provide an abstract description of that "something," but we ourselves, as the observers, are not able to fully see the "something" for exactly what the "something" is. Lastly, a completely different way to understand a theory is to fall into the group of people who are called *instrumentalists*. For this particular group, a theory is a very mysterious thing indeed, because a theory can really only serve as a model for predicting some states of affairs in the world. Here, a theory has moved from being a description of something to being a model for predicting something or demonstrating the usefulness of something. For this reason, *instrumentalists* might even say that "reality" cannot be known or perhaps the notion of "reality" is meaningless. For them, science provides opportunities to model the world, but we'll never know if our models are accurate descriptions of reality as reality is.

Michael Polanyi (b. 1891, d. 1976), who was a Hungarian chemist and philosopher, had a great way of explaining the notion of a theory. In his book *Personal Knowledge* (1962), Polanyi defines a theory as follows: "A theory is something other than myself. It may be set out on paper as a system of rules, and it is the more truly a theory the more completely it can be put down in such terms."[7] Polanyi also remarked, "Indeed, all theory may be regarded as a kind of map extended over space and time."[8] If we try to understand what a theory is by using Polanyi's definition it doesn't seem to matter if we are classical realists, critical realists, or instrumentalists. The important point is that a theory is something other than ourselves and we can rely on it to help us as we move through the unknown. If you'd like, go ahead and pick one of the groups—classical realists, critical realists, or instrumentalists—for yourself to fit into. If you'd rather not pick right now, that's fine, too. There will be opportunities to make other decisions like this one throughout our adventure.

The 20th century philosopher of science Sir Karl Popper (b. 1902, d. 1994) explains that even if a theory ends up being false, the theory was still a great achievement.[9] A theory that ends up being false can provide us with an opportunity to make some changes to the old theory and then develop a new theory! Scientific theories need to be tested. It is important that we can test a theory to make sure the theory *accurately* predicts real life states of affairs in the world. For a theory to be tested, Popper says a theory should have the *potential* to be found to be false. How can a theory have the potential to be found to be false? Well, let's say we have a theory and we would like to test it. We need to have some physical phenomenon that our theory cannot explain or solve. We need to know what that phenomenon is ahead of time.[10] We perform a real life experiment that is based on our theory. Now, here is the catch: If the particular phenomenon (that we knew initially could not be explained by our theory) ends up being demonstrated in real life by our *theory*-based experiment, we know that our *theory* was actually false. This may sound a bit strange at first, but, if you read over the previous few sentences a few times, I think you will soon get the idea. The theory was found to be false, because the theory appeared to demonstrate a real life phenomenon that we know it actually cannot demonstrate! So, the theory does not accurately predict real life states of affairs in the world. Of course we don't just rule out a theory if one single time it messes up (there can be random mishaps). However, if the theory *repeatedly* messes up, we know that something isn't right.

The following is an example of how a real life scientific theory has the potential to be found to be false: Atomic theory was suggested initially in the early 19 century and then developed further in the early 20th century by Ernest Rutherford and Niels Bohr. Atomic theory provides a structural picture of the atom, the smallest piece of a chemical element. Atomic theory allows us to predict the mass of an atom. Atomic theory does this by telling us the number and types of subatomic (small) particles which exist inside an atom. Let's suppose that one day a new chemical element is discovered (sometimes this does happen). Let's call the new chemical element "Religio." Religio is a solid at room temperature. We don't yet know the mass of an atom of Religio. Unfortunately, the chemical scale in our laboratory broke and had to go out for maintenance. We really need to figure out the mass of an atom of Religio today! We decide to apply atomic theory. Thanks to our advanced chemical tools of the 21st century (which are much less prone to breaking than chemical scales), we figure out that Religio has 135 subatomic particles of varying types. That is great. Now, using our knowledge of how many subatomic particles Religio has (135), we combine that knowledge with *atomic theory*. Using our experiment, which is based on atomic theory, we calculate that the mass of a single atom of Religio is 145.3 amu (atomic mass units). This is good, because atomic theory has provided us with a useful alternative for discovering knowledge while our chemical scale was being repaired.

About a week later, the broken scale is repaired and returned to our laboratory. We figure we might as well double check the mass of a single atom of Religio by weighing the solid form of Religio on the scale. We weigh Religio on the scale. To our surprise, we get a mass of 175.2 amu. We weigh a different sample of Religio on the scale and we get a mass of 175.4 amu. Finally, we weigh a completely different sample of Religio on the scale and we get a mass of 175.1 amu. Something is not right: none of these measurements are close to 145.3 amu. Chances are the scale itself is not the problem, because we weighed three different samples of Religio at different times on the scale and every time we got roughly the same mass (about 175 amu). From atomic theory, we thought that any mass other than 145.3 amu could not be the mass of a single atom of Religio, because from atomic theory we discovered that the mass of a single atom of Religio is 145.3 amu. I'm afraid, folks, that we just found atomic theory to be false. We have a physical phenomenon that atomic theory cannot explain or solve—atomic theory cannot explain or solve why the mass of a single atom of Religio is, in fact, about 175 amu. Now, a big disclaimer: You of course know that I made up this example, and that a good scientific theory, like atomic theory, cannot just be found to be false if a single time it messes up. However, this example demonstrates, philosophically, how scientific theories must have the *potential* to be found to be false. That is how scientific theories are tested. There will always remain the possibility that, someday, a theory that we all know and love could be found to be false. Remember: scientific theories are descriptions of physical reality or useful models for reality; scientific theories are not truths. Sometimes if a scientific theory has been working well for a long time—explaining natural phenomena and accurately predicting new knowledge—we might decide to call the theory a *law*, as in the *law of gravity*. However, for the most part, we retain the term *theory* to describe the form of scientific knowledge.

A brief digression for literary-minded folks (and everyone else): In Aldous Huxley's novel *Antic Hay* (1923), a group of bohemian artists, who are more or less dissatisfied with life, discuss the possibility that science and art, and religion and philosophy, are all different human ways of expressing one "reality" which is beyond human comprehension. The characters, Lypiatt and Shearwater, describe the frustrations they experience when scientists interpret science as truth and not as theory. The character Lypiatt says,

> 'The physicists have formulated their laws, which are after all no more than stammering provisional theories about a part of it [reality]. The physiologists are penetrating into the secrets of life, psychologists into the mind. And we artists are trying to say what is revealed to us about the moral nature, the personality of that reality, which is the universe.'[11]

In response, the character Shearwater says,

> 'Quite right about the chemists and physicists. They're always trying to pretend that they're nearer the truth than we are. They take their crude theories as facts and try to make us accept them when we're dealing with life. Oh, they are sacred, their theories. Laws of Nature they call them; and they talk about their known truths and our romantic biological fancies. What a fuss they make when we talk about life! Bloody fools!'[12]

Huxley wrote in the early 1920s when traditional standards and conventions were being questioned (after its publication *Antic Hay* was burned in Cairo), but interestingly the situation that Lypiatt and Shearwater describe about the sciences is not far off from real life. As a former engineering student, I can say from experience that chemistry, physics, and other subjects like these, are taught in universities as if the knowledges passed on in those classes, from teacher to student, are statements of truths (some science or engineering students may disagree, but I think most would agree that the term *theory* is hardly ever used in university or college classes). In actuality, it would be more helpful to everyone if the simple clarification was made that the knowledges gained in the science or engineering disciplines are not truths, but are the best theories that we have for a time. In the future, new theories may replace old theories. This is what it means for scientific knowledge to be *open to change*.

To recap once more, in our adventure, we seek a common ground in science by understanding that scientific theories are not truths, but scientific theories are descriptions of reality or useful models for reality. The distinction between *knowledge* and *truth* is important—as human beings, we do not possess a form of knowledge that would be needed (whatever that form would be) to say that a claim of knowledge is the *truth*. In fact, from Thomas Kuhn's perspective, there is not one type of "truth." Instead the "truth" is dependent on the paradigm that a person is working under. How might there be more than one "truth" about the world? Even if you find this idea completely bizarre, consider this analogy for a moment: What about time? In regards to stating the most "correct" time in the world at a given moment, there isn't one most "correct" time, but many most "correct" times which depend on which time zone a person is residing in. While it can be 12 a.m. at one location in the world (Toronto, Canada), it is 6 a.m. at another location (Frankfurt, Germany), or 4 p.m. at another (Sydney, Australia) and so forth. Any one of these possible times is "correct" even though they are actually all different. Whether or not this example is really analogous to the idea of multiple "truths," I don't know; however, the example of time zones does help to put into perspective how there can be more than one of something. The time zone example also shows how *context* is always important. In the case of telling the time, a time zone provides the context for why one particular time is stated as the "correct" time even though in other time zones (other contexts) different times will be stated as the "correct" times. Context is also important in how we think about the notion of *truth*. In the case of science, we have learned that paradigms can change. If a paradigm can change then our context for understanding the world can also change. If paradigms can change, then "truth" can also change . . . at least if you are a Kuhnian, a follower of Thomas Kuhn's philosophy; however, that is up to you! There are different "truth" camps of people and at this point in our adventure you can choose to set up your tent wherever you like. Do be advised, however, that if you choose to be a Kuhnian (I, myself, tend to favor this view), your very decision to choose to be a Kuhnian constitutes a choice of one particular paradigm: the paradigm that *Thomas Kuhn's philosophy is "correct."* So, the truth of the statement *Thomas Kuhn's philosophy is "correct"* depends on you believing that this statement is right. Do you *believe* this statement is right? Aha, what a suitable gateway to return to our discussion of *belief*, which we left behind previously when we focused on *knowledge*.

NOTES

1. Sir David Brewster, *Memoirs of the Life, Writings, and Discoveries of Sir Isaac Newton*, 1855.
2. Thomas S. Kuhn, *The Structure of Scientific Revolutions*, 4th ed. (Chicago: The University of Chicago Press, 2012), 10.
3. Kuhn, *The Structure of Scientific Revolutions*, 23.
4. Ibid., 10.
5. Ibid., 11.
6. Ibid.
7. Michael Polanyi, *Personal Knowledge: Towards a Post-Critical Philosophy* (1962; repr., Chicago: The University of Chicago Press, 1974), 4.
8. Polanyi, *Personal Knowledge*, 4.
9. Karl R. Popper, *Conjectures and Refutations: The Growth of Scientific Knowledge* (1963; repr., New York: Routledge, 2002), 190.
10. Karl R. Popper, *The Logic of Scientific Discovery* (1959; repr., New York: Routledge, 2002), 95–96.
11. Aldous Huxley, *Antic Hay* (1923; repr., London: Vintage, 2004), 57.
12. Huxley, *Antic Hay*, 57.

Chapter Three

Beliefs

In the previous chapter, we learned that a scientific epistemology (a scientific *form of knowledge*) governs the search for knowledge of the natural world and the engineering of the world's materials. I used the philosophies of Thomas Kuhn and Karl Popper to show how a scientific epistemology is a type of framework for knowledge that is *open to change*. The wonderful thing about a scientific epistemology is that it is so much more than simply a means to obtain information about states of affairs in the world. Yes, that is important, but a scientific epistemology is also an *attitude of mind* or *a way of life*. It is an attitude of being open to modification of one's world view—an attitude of accepting that all knowledge is corrigible, which means that all knowledge has the potential to be corrected or tweaked. Acknowledging this type of attitude of mind is the very definition of *rationality* (*rational*) itself. A large part of our adventure is to develop an attitude of mind that allows room for us to make changes to our world views and re-evaluate the nature of our own knowledges and beliefs. The Scottish professor Ninian Smart (b. 1927, d. 2001), who was largely responsible for encouraging us to take a step "outside" religion so that we can see what is happening "inside" religion, says the following about worldviews (he combines *world* and *view* into one term *worldview*): "The modern study of worldviews helps illuminate worldviews, of course, both traditional and secular, which are such an engine of both continuity and change, and therefore it explores feelings and ideas and tries to understand what exists inside the heads of people. What people believe is an important aspect of reality whether or not what they believe is true."[1] An interesting distinction here between things we might experience as reality and things we believe to be true. Another aspect of epistemology (our term for the *form of knowledge*) is to use the methods of science (some of which we've already seen) or the methods of religion (coming up soon) to distinguish between the things we believe are true, called *justified beliefs*, and the things that might be true but we cannot say with certainty whether or not we should believe they are true—these are called *non-justified beliefs*. However, both of these types of beliefs are perhaps a part of reality, because both types of beliefs—justified beliefs and non-justified beliefs—influence our lives, providing us with meaning and purpose in life. Sometimes it is not so much a question of whether or not we can show that a belief is justified, but rather the importance lies in whether a belief will contribute to a meaningful and purposeful life.

I almost wasn't going to include the previous sentence (the last sentence in the preceding paragraph) in this book. I am glad that I did include it, but I almost did not include it because the content of that sentence is problematic, perhaps even dangerous, even though it is an accurate description of how "reality" is often understood. The problem is that deciding where the border line falls between justified beliefs and non-justified beliefs has not been a peaceful enterprise, but one wrought with turmoil and struggle, usually at the expense of people's lives. In the 21st century this is less of a problem now that people from various religious backgrounds are living together and sharing the same jobs and studying in the same schools. We are beginning more and more to understand that we don't have to specify any one particular institution or culture as being the only way in which healthy human values can flourish (in the West, these values have been called Judaeo-Christian values). However, let us briefly jump back 700 years or so, to the fourteenth century, when if you claimed a belief—usually the claim that you had an experience from beyond this world—and religious authorities didn't agree with you, you could pretty much expect to be executed as a heretic. There were other people, called witches, who did not claim to have any unusual experiences, but were accused by others of having experiences that arose from a demonic realm (the Devil). Those people didn't have much luck either and were quickly burned at the stake. The feminist philosopher Grace Jantzen (b. 1948, d. 2006), known for her work on religious mysticism, explains that although some men were executed for witchcraft, we cannot deny that most accused of witchcraft were women.[2] Jantzen's work focused on power and gender and how those factors influenced whether a person's belief claim was accepted by others, or not. Witch hunts continued until the seventeenth century, and then gradually declined, possibly because of a new emphasis on scientific rationalism when it became more difficult for narrow-minded people to suggest that women were morally inferior to men. Or, as Jantzen proposes, changes in social views of gender in the seventeenth century (science and philosophy were viewed as "masculine") meant that witch hunts no longer had a purpose as gender roles could now be controlled through other structures of society.[3] The example of heretics and witches is a particular instance, captured in a moment in time when it was not very clear on how one might adjudicate the legitimacy of knowledge claims or beliefs. We are, of course, far removed from such a time, but this example demonstrates how life can go seriously haywire if we are not careful to really consider how we separate justified beliefs from non-justified beliefs. If we do not wish to draw a border line between these two types of beliefs, that is fine, but we then have to provide everyone with the freedom to claim whatever beliefs they choose (so long as no one is being harmed in the process). If we do desire to draw a border line between justified beliefs and non-justified beliefs, we had better make sure that our framework for adjudicating beliefs is a good one. In fact, this is what has already been done in places of modern, Western research and study. It is widely accepted that a *scientific epistemology*, as we have discussed, is the best framework available to us to separate justified beliefs from non-justified beliefs.

Scientific research is designed to gather justified beliefs (knowledge) about states of affairs in the world. As such, scientific research relies on evidence observed from the natural world, so that knowledge gained from an experiment can be shown to be justified. When I was an engineering chemistry student, my thesis project was working to improve the flexibility of gels, composed of long chains of molecules, with the intention that the gels could (some day) be used as structures to grow artificial cartilage cells.[4] I had to run some tests on the gels to see if the results of my research had actually made the gels more flexible. These tests were very tedious to complete. For every gel that I tested I had to run the same test three different times at three different locations on each gel. Then, I would average my results and calculate the standard deviation for each set of data. The reason that I had to run the tests so many times for the same gel was to make sure that my results were consistent. It was not enough to simply run the test one time for each gel, because it was possible that the one test would be faulty for some reason. By running the test multiple times and then averaging all of the results, I was able to ensure that every test was giving me roughly the same result. In this way, the knowledge I claimed to have discovered was justified and the conclusions that I formed were convincing. Scientific epistemology utilizes experimental research and elements of the philosophy of science, such as the philosophies described by Thomas Kuhn and Karl Popper, who we learned about previously. Scientific epistemology ensures that knowledge gained from an experiment is equivalent to justified belief. All in all, we have seen how the use of epistemology (the *form of knowledge*) is very important in scientific life. Now, with all of this in mind, I wonder: how important is epistemology in religious life?

I mentioned before that it is difficult to define the word *science* so that everyone agrees with the definition. It is even more difficult to define the word *religion* so that everyone agrees with the definition. You may already have your own definition of *religion* in mind. If so, that is fine. If not, here are some possibilities for a definition of *religion*:

1. Religion is the corporate or public expression of one's faith, as displayed in a community of people who share the same beliefs.
2. From the etymology of the word *religion*, which is the Latin word *religio*, a verb, meaning *I bind together*, religion is a situation where a group of people gather together or a situation where one person is bound in relationship to another.
3. Religion is *belief* about a trans-empirical world.

The third definition—religion is *belief* about a trans-empirical world—suits the purpose of our adventure quite well. We distinguish between the adjectives *empirical* and *trans-empirical*. Let me explain what this means: Science is an *empirical* activity. *Empirical* means we have to observe something in the physical world if we want to say that something is a description of reality or that something is a model for reality. Usually we read the mass of an object on a scale, we assess the acidity of a solution using a chemical test, or we read the temperature off a thermometer. These are all *empirical* ways that we can describe or model reality. *Trans-empirical* is very different from *empirical*. *Trans-empirical* is "outside" the empirical or beyond the empirical. In the adjective *trans-empirical*, the prefix *trans* is taken from *transcendence*, a commonly used word in religious life, which means a situation that is "across" the visible world (*trans* itself is a Latin word which translates into English as *across*—e.g. a *trans*-atlantic flight goes *across* the Atlantic Ocean). In the case of a trans-empirical world, we are talking about a reality that we cannot describe and a reality that we cannot model. A trans-empirical world is "outside" the visible world or "across" the visible world. We cannot see a trans-empirical world. Scales, chemical tests, or thermometers are not going to help us here. All that we have in the trans-empirical world is our instincts and . . . our faith.

One of my professors in Toronto, Donald Wiebe, in his book *The Irony of Theology and the Nature of Religious Thought* (1991), explains *religion* in this way: "Religion, that is, will be taken to consist of the stories of transcendence [a trans-empirical world]; of another realm of reality; of superhuman/supernatural being(s) that have the power to help (or to harm) humankind."[5] Wiebe's definition is useful to us, because it provides us with some common themes for *religion* regardless of any one particular religious tradition. At this point, I am not even going to mention the names of religious traditions, because, just as I did not mention the various types of scientific or engineering disciplines, the purpose of our adventure is not to focus on the various types of religious traditions. Instead we are talking about *belief* and, more specifically, belief about a trans-empirical world, which is a world beyond the empirical world of the sciences. Knowledge claims about an empirical world, such as the "world" of biology, can be proven or disproven, using methods described by the philosophy of science. For example, Karl Popper's idea that a scientific theory must be tested and have the potential to be found to be false is included in the description of an empirical world. As mentioned, a trans-empirical world is a world that we cannot describe and cannot model. Interestingly, we also cannot prove or disprove the existence of a trans-empirical world. If we are religious people, *belief* about a trans-empirical world contributes every day to the formation of meaning and purpose in our lives.

What is going on here? One of the issues that generates our need as human beings to experience *belief* about a trans-empirical world (rather than deferring only to the empirical world) is that we will, someday, die. Belief is a way for us to project our human thoughts and emotions, our greatest hopes and fears, beyond our finite human existence. About this, Wiebe rightly observes, "The recognition of human limitation—of finitude—in face of the inexorable processes of nature that eventuate in death, and the transcending of those limitations by postulating (recognizing/assuming) the existence of a superhuman source of power on which humans can draw, is what religion is essentially all about."[6] The word *postulate* (expressed as the verb *postulating* in the preceding quotation) is related to the word *belief*. As religious people, we postulate (suggest/hypothesize) the existence of a superhuman power. Our postulation is a *belief* of the existence of a superhuman power. We cannot verify whether or not a superhuman power actually exists. So, what do we do? Well, it is really up to each of us to decide what we choose to do. We will explore some implications of this as we begin to fill our roles as adjudicators. For now, I will say that, in my own opinion, it is not the best idea to utilize the activity of a superhuman power as an explanation for why we possess religious knowledge. If we are using the framework of scientific knowledge as our model for religious knowledge (scientific knowledge is open to change and can be corrected through experience; we would like religious knowledge to function in the same way), then any agent whose existence we cannot prove—including a god or gods—is best left out. A person might wonder, then, why are we even talking about religious knowledge in the first place? My response to that concern would be that even though we *cannot prove* the existence of a superhuman power in a trans-empirical world, we also *cannot disprove* the existence of a superhuman power in a trans-empirical world. Whether a trans-empirical world is for you a world of a single god or goddess, many gods or goddesses, or more generally a world of superhuman power is not so relevant. Whatever a trans-empirical world is for you, is up to you! In this adventure we are collectively concerned with asking: i) How do we makes sense of our postulation that a trans-empirical world exists? and ii) How are we going to adjudicate the legitimacy of a trans-empirical world?

I have suggested we might think twice before using a superhuman power as an explanation for religious knowledge. However, it is the case that we can receive meaning and purpose in our lives from *believing* that our postulation—of the existence of a superhuman power—is a legitimate postulation. (There are two forms of belief here: our postulations themselves are beliefs, but we also have to believe that our postulations are right.) In the 21st century when knowledge claims are often questioned and an account must be given for why a particular knowledge claim is thought to be legitimate, religious knowledge (e.g. belief of "God") is severely under attack. Perhaps this attack is justified or perhaps it is not. At any rate, unlike scientific knowledge that we discussed previously, religious knowledge is a type of knowledge that does *not* seem to be open to change. Religious knowledge, in its traditional sense, does not create space for a person to possess an attitude of mind allowing for modification of one's world view. Religious knowledge cannot be tested. This is the dividing line between scientific knowledge and religious knowledge. Scientific and religious exercises constitute different types of knowledges, and they are very different types of knowledge indeed. They must not be confused. If religious knowledge desires the special status of scientific knowledge (an attitude of being open to change), then religious knowledge must accept the benchmark of scientific knowledge, which is observed/tested experience. If religious knowledge does not desire the special status of scientific knowledge, then religious knowledge is free to choose its own benchmark (whatever that would be) for adjudicating purposes; however, it may then sacrifice the special reputation toward learning held by scientific knowledge. Since the purpose of a scientific epistemology is to provide a learning format where ideas can be proposed, tested, and then accepted or thrown out, scientific knowledge and learning go hand in hand. Learning is best accomplished when there are opportunities to modify or tweak the knowledges and beliefs that a person possesses.

A pro-religion person might ask the question: isn't religious knowledge also tested, because I can wait and see whether or not my religious knowledge helps me to have a better life and that in itself is a type of tested experience? I'm afraid this is a weak point and amounts to nothing more than playing with words. There's no doubt that religious people have "religious experiences," but the problem is that these experiences are often not repeatable and even if they are repeatable they cannot be measured numerically or reproduced artificially in a laboratory setting. How do we experimentally test a scientific theory? To test a scientific theory, the results of scientific knowledge are repeated during an experiment, they are often measured numerically (or modeled using equations), they are reproduced under artificial conditions in a laboratory, and they are open to criticism. We need to have all of these options available to us so that we can adequately test knowledge. If these options are not available, we can't be sure that we have adequately tested knowledge. Even if you had an experience that you believe was a religious experience, how can you be sure of its source? Was it a dream? Were you in the presence of others and a collective vibe of excitement travelled through your group? Had you been drinking some wine? Perhaps your experience did come from God, but how are you going to test that? You can't actually know for sure. You can *believe* your experience came from God (I'm not saying you can't believe it), but you can't *know* it. To hammer the point home, if opportunities to be rational—opportunities for learning from tested experience—do not exist within a person's world view, then how does that person expect to learn anything new (and call it *knowledge*) while functioning within that particular world view? Go ahead and call whatever you want *belief*. Just don't abuse the word *knowledge*. If you really have the need to use the word *knowledge* when describing your religious experiences, then call those experiences "religious knowledge," as we have been doing in this adventure.

A brief disclaimer is in order: You may be concerned that as the author I have placed science in a privileged position over religion (or perhaps you like it that way). Indeed, during the initial planning for my doctoral degree project, which is related to the topics in this book, some of my friends and professors (who are very caring people) were a bit concerned that I was placing scientific knowledge in a privileged position over religious knowledge. Yes, I have done that. I have done that, because it is my sense that only after the benefits of scientific knowledge are discussed can the merits of religious knowledge really be investigated. My intention is that this book reaches a wide audience of readers from varied and diverse backgrounds. In setting up the previous chapters in the ways that I have, my intention was to demonstrate how scientific knowledge is special and unique. Now, having done that, I have provided all of us with some scholarly clout to take on the question of how do we adjudicate the legitimacy of religious knowledge? If I had not first recognized scientific knowledge as privileged, I probably would not possess the qualifications to continue as your leader in our quest to become adjudicators. Now that the scientific position is fully acknowledged, we can move on to better and brighter things. This would be a good time for each of us to take a brief moment to pause and decide which of these options we would like to adopt moving forward:

1. Do we desire religious knowledge to be *open to change* just as scientific knowledge is open to change?
2. Do we desire to accept that, unlike scientific knowledge, religious knowledge does *not* seem to be open to change and should remain that way?

On some level, the choice of which of these options you choose will determine what kind of adjudicator you will later become. Again, like all decisions in this book, that decision is up to you. It is your decision. Not mine or anyone else's. It is yours. You can also decide now and then change your mind later, if you like.

Take a moment to think about a story from your own life that involves some kind of scientific knowledge, religious knowledge, or a combination of both. In the medical sciences, perhaps it was scientific knowledge that helped you to get better from an illness, or experience the benefits of a minor surgery, such as treating cataracts or having your tonsils removed. In the engineering disciplines, perhaps it was scientific knowledge that helped you develop a new chemical filtration product which made it easier for people in third world countries to receive access to clean water. In your spiritual life, perhaps it was religious knowledge (or spiritual knowledge) that played a significant role in how you dealt with the challenges of growing up and then starting your own career. Perhaps in the company of your family, it was religious knowledge that helped you to confront the emotions you experienced when someone who you loved died. Perhaps you include both scientific knowledge and religious knowledge in your life, creating an interesting (and sometimes confusing) paradox. Perhaps you would like to share your story with a friend, colleague, family member, or someone who you trust. You can also keep your story to yourself if you like. The important thing is to spend some time reflecting on how scientific knowledge or religious knowledge or a combination of both might influence your life.

As your leader in this adventure, here is a story from my life which may help to clarify my own position on the problem of distinguishing scientific knowledge from religious knowledge: We have seen how the question of the legitimacy of religious knowledge or the legitimacy of any other *type* of knowledge that is not scientific knowledge, is a complicated question. There are some types of knowledge that cannot be classified as either scientific or religious. These types of knowledge are just too "grey" for us to say, one way or the other, what exactly they are. When I was a child I had a neurological condition where my face and arms made physical movements that I could not control. Mainstream doctors, whose training was based on scientific knowledge (medicine), were unable to provide a treatment that would heal me from this condition. Despite all the years of previous neurological research that had occurred prior to my childhood in the 1990s, the best that doctors could do for me was to prescribe a single drug which didn't do anything to alleviate my condition. As an adult looking back on my childhood experience, I acknowledge there are still many diseases where treatments have not yet been discovered. I also recognize that scientific knowledge has gloriously provided successful treatments for many pathetic diseases—this is a good thing. Still, though, with my own childhood situation, scientific knowledge wasn't good enough. I don't think my particular condition was even diagnosable—my condition was just too "grey" for any kind of scientific study.

By the time I began high school a person who worked in my hometown had healed me. I can't say exactly what this person did. His professional practice involved a series of natural health treatments, which, I suppose, some would call alternative medicine. The first thing he did was to have me eliminate all meat and dairy products from my meals for three months. I remember being eager to go along with this. I think this strategy was to get my body back into a kind of primitive state; to "shock" my body into a state that would be more receptive to healing. After about four years of natural treatment, the condition was gone. I experienced the condition gradually decrease and then go away entirely. I don't know if there is anyone else in the world who does the particular healing work this person does. As an adult I asked this person whether he would apply the same treatment he applied in my case if someone else came to him with a condition similar to what my condition was? His answer to my question was a "grey" answer. This didn't surprise me. His answer was something along the lines of that each person's treatment is specific to the situation of each person. There isn't a single generic "treatment" that can be applied to everyone with similar health conditions.

In terms of "knowledge," what happened to me as a child? Yes, scientific knowledge (mainstream medicine) failed me. Did I experience religious knowledge? No, I don't think so (it wasn't as though a superhuman agent came down to earth and healed me). However, I experienced something. There's no question about that. So, what was it? Whether or not the treatments that healed me could be explained using tested scientific theories, I don't know. I suppose it is possible, but that would probably never happen, because scientific knowledge, as we've said, needs to be measured numerically and have the capability of being reproduced artificially in a laboratory. Nothing in the healing process of my childhood illness could be measured numerically or reproduced in a laboratory. Nothing in that healing process was open to critical discussion, which is a regular benchmark of scientific knowledge. The *type* of knowledge that was used to heal me was neither scientific nor religious. Perhaps in some way it drew on both of these, but it was something different entirely. Whatever it was continues to intrigue me to this day—not in a confusing way, but in a mysterious way. It's not that I think about my childhood experience every day, but, if I recall it (as I did when I wrote this book), it causes me to remember that I can't ever rule out the possibility that other *types* of knowledge might exist—perhaps types of *private* knowledges.

Thank you for reading my story. I wanted to include it to help clarify better my own position on scientific and religious knowledges—I think that, ultimately, they are both very "grey." (They are also all that we have and most of the time they do seem to be useful to us.) On some level, my childhood experience probably plays a role in my unconscious when I wonder about human knowledges and beliefs. Maybe that's another reason why I wanted to write this book and be your leader in this adventure. At any rate, we have a lot more to cover, so I had better stop telling stories and get on with it. I do hope you are able to think about your own story involving scientific knowledge or religious knowledge or both. If I was your friend, I would be interested in hearing your story. Perhaps there is a person who you will share your story with. The next and final chapter of this section is called *Belief as Trust*. We are going to refine what we learned in this current chapter on *beliefs* and then add in some new ideas. I think you are going to find it very interesting. . . .

NOTES

1. Ninian Smart, *Worldviews: Crosscultural Exploration of Human Beliefs* (Upper Saddle River: Prentice-Hall, Inc., 2000), 1–2.

2. Grace Jantzen, *Power, Gender and Christian Mysticism* (New York: Cambridge University Press, 1995), 265.

3. Jantzen, *Power, Gender and Christian Mysticism*, 276.

4. Andrew Ralls Woodward, "Biocompatible Hydrogels of Methacrylated Glycol Chitosan: A Focus on Improving Their Flexibility and Degradation Using Star-poly(trimethylene carbonate-co-D,L-lactide) triacrylate" (Bachelor's thesis, Queen's University, 2010), 3.

5. Donald Wiebe, *The Irony of Theology and the Nature of Religious Thought* (Montreal: McGill-Queen's University Press, 1991), 33.

6. Wiebe, *The Irony of Theology and the Nature of Religious Thought*, 33.

Chapter Four

Belief as Trust

We will soon move ahead to the next phase of our adventure—Part II, *Scientific and Religious People*. Before moving ahead we need to spend a bit more time exploring the complexity of *belief*. Indeed, if we would like to experience life as scientific and religious people (I suspect there are a lot of us who would like to do that), we really need to understand the complexity involved in believing. (Like anything that we learn for the first time, something new is complex only at the beginning. Eventually, what seemed to be new and confusing, ends up becoming fun and easy.) During this stage of our adventure, I will introduce to you the philosophy of religious belief and the philosophy of belief in general. In regards to believing, the fact is there is not one way to believe, but there are various ways to believe; there is not one type of belief, but there are various types of belief. Here I am not talking about beliefs about different superhuman agents (gods) or beliefs that arise from different religious traditions (although we will touch on those ideas in the next section). Rather, here I am talking about what is *happening* inside the *thoughts* of our human minds when we *believe*; what kinds of *commitments* are we making inside our thoughts when we *believe*. These commitments might be commitments to a god or commitments to another human being. If we are religious people, it seems that most of us will say, "I (we) believe *in* God." However, what about statements such as, "I (we) believe *that* God exists" or "I (we) *possess* a belief *about* God"? Are these various statements equivalent or are they different? (In these examples, I am using the term *God*, but *Allah* or the name of another mythological superhuman agent—*Zeus, Attis, Adonis*, etc.—could be substituted here.) Using epistemology (our term for the *form of knowledge*), we can distinguish between i) belief expressed as a belief claim and ii) belief as *trust*. For some, this may amount to a minor point. I acknowledge that most of us travel throughout our religious lives without ever a need to consider a difference between belief claims and belief as *trust*. However, there may be some of us who would appreciate an explanation and this whole matter about belief claims and trust does make for an interesting conversation at a cocktail party! Donald Wiebe points out to us that, with belief, we have two options: either we understand belief using epistemology or we understand belief without using epistemology.[1] Although both options are acceptable, the difference is quite striking! Let's find out why. . . .

To understand belief using epistemology (using the *form of knowledge*), as adjudicators, we ask ourselves the question: what exactly is the object of our belief—what is the "reality" *about* which we *possess* a belief? Like knowledge, which is directed toward an object, (e.g. an atom, a cell, or an abstract scientific theory), it seems that belief also needs to be directed toward an object (at least most of the time). Yes, I hear you—I hear you saying that the object which a belief is directed toward is the object of God, expressed in the statement "I (we) believe *that* God exists." This is a good point and I certainly don't mean to diminish its credibility. However, let's pause for a moment and ask ourselves this question: was there not something else, some other type of belief, already present in our lives, which led us (perhaps unconsciously) to express the statement "I (we) believe *that* God exists"? And, if so, what is this other belief? I think most of us would agree that the statement "I (we) believe *that* God exists" did not just arise out of nowhere. There was something else going on before—something which led us to make that statement. Whatever was going on before may be, for lack of a better word, *trust*. In Latin, *trust* is *fiducia* and *belief* is *fides*. Throughout the centuries, a convention developed in theological schools where the Latin words *fiducia* and *fides* were used to distinguish two different types of beliefs. In English, these two types of beliefs are: i) belief expressed as a belief claim (*fides*) and ii) belief as trust (*fiducia*).

The distinction between a belief claim and belief as trust becomes apparent when we decide whether we would like to understand belief using epistemology or without epistemology. As mentioned previously, epistemology is about making a knowledge claim about states of affairs in the world, whether a knowledge claim in science or a *belief claim* in religion. So, when we use the philosophical tool of epistemology, available to us in our arsenal of all philosophical and theological tools, we are dealing with a knowledge claim about some object of "reality"—either an object we *know* to exist (e.g. an atom, through scientific testing) or an object we *believe* to exist (e.g. a god, through religious experience). When we express our belief as a *belief claim* (which is similar to expressing a knowledge claim), we are in fact saying, "we believe *that* God exists." We aren't saying, "we believe *in* God" (although in church the words often come out that way). The statement "we believe *in* God" is really beyond the grasp of our ability as humans to make a belief claim, because that statement seems to suggest we have a personal experience of God, as if we were God. In religious life what we are actually saying is that we *possess* belief *about* God. This type of human belief is a belief claim—"we believe *that* God exists"—which in Latin is *fides*. I also note that in many religions there are opportunities for religious followers to experience personal knowledge of God—something where the religious follower enters into a relationship with the life of God. It seems to me this type of personal experience is still, primarily, a belief expressed in the form of a belief claim—i.e. the statement "I believe *that* I possess a personal experience of God." Personal experience of God is, in itself, an object of belief, existing separate from the life of the religious follower. On this point, if you would like to disagree with me, that's fine. (It is important that we keep our minds open to alternative perspectives—attitudes of being open to change—and are not afraid to agree or disagree with one another as we see fit.) The so-called religious mystics of the past (and present) would probably disagree with me when I say that any personal experience of God exists separate from the religious follower. From what I understand, in religious mysticism, there is a sense that the "reality" of God has been intertwined with the "reality" of the religious follower (mystic), to the point that the religious follower loses his or her own sense of individual consciousness. In this case, it would seem the personal experience of God, as an object of belief, does not exist separately from the religious follower, but in fact coalesces in some way with the human life of the religious follower. To use our previous terminology about empirical and trans-empirical worlds, it appears that in religious mysticism the visible, empirical world coalesces with the invisible, trans-empirical world, making the "boundaries" which separate these worlds blurred or even non-existent. It's an interesting thought. I just don't know how far we want to move in that direction. After all, as with any religious phenomenon, reports of religious mysticism cannot be tested. Experiences of religious mysticism belong to the individuals who report having such experiences; those experiences are rarely (if ever) repeated and cannot be artificially reproduced. Nevertheless people from various religious traditions do report having these experiences.

What role, then, does the concept of belief as *trust* (*fiducia*) play? Well, as adjudicators, we also have the option to understand belief without using epistemology (without the *form of knowledge*). Leaving epistemology aside for a moment, we discover that belief claims do in fact depend first upon *trust*, which in Latin is *fiducia*. So, *fiducia*, the so-called unconscious or implicit condition of trust, is already present, existing in our lives before we even get to the point of saying, "I (we) believe *that* God exists." *Fiducia* is the type of belief we express when we say, "we *trust in* God," alluding to a personal, intimate knowledge of God and a knowledge already present. With *fiducia*, we are not merely making a statement "we believe *that* God exists."

Rather, we are saying, "we *trust in* God," or, to put it more bluntly, "we have a personal experience of God." Whatever this personal experience amounts to, I cannot say. You might decide to connect this personal experience with the ideas of religious mysticism. As your own adjudicator, you can think about belief as trust (*fiducia*) in whatever way you like. In this chapter I present us with some possibilities for how belief as *trust* may be meaningful in our everyday lives on earth. Again, this is not *trust* as an object of a belief claim, but rather this *trust* is a human condition, a state, or a way of life. Perhaps we are born with it or perhaps we die with it, but either way it is already here. It seems we cannot get away from it. Yes, we may go one step further, toward expressing a belief claim, saying, "we believe *that* God exists," or "we believe *that* other people exist," or even "we believe *that* we ourselves exist." However, we cannot take those additional steps if the condition of *trust*, itself, was not already present. The condition of trust is the fuel which allows us to eventually formulate the beliefs existing in our human minds into belief claims, such as the various belief claims stated in this chapter.

For the record, *trusting in* other people or *trusting in* ourselves are also other types of trust. Quite rightly, in life we have the options of trusting in other people or trusting in ourselves. It seems that we might be wise to include trust in ourselves and trust in our fellow human beings along with our trust in God. Are perhaps all of these types of trust in fact *one trust* which is a trust in humankind? Or, a trust in creation? A trust in life itself? Or, a trust in the outcomes of possessing a life of faith? Our goal in this adventure is to become adjudicators of human knowledges and beliefs. We are well on our way to fulfilling that goal and I like to remind us of that goal as we progress. In this chapter *Belief as Trust* we learned about how, with or without epistemology, there are different types of beliefs in the world: Some beliefs are belief claims where we explicitly talk about an object of belief. In contrast, belief as *trust* is just there and we cannot get away from it. Whenever you are presented in your life with a belief, you can ask yourselves: what *type* of belief is this? That question might help you to decide if the belief is, for you, a legitimate belief (a justified belief) and also whether the belief is a belief claim *or* belief as trust? You can also ask yourselves what kinds of commitments you are making when you decide whether or not a belief claim is legitimate? Are you making a commitment to a god or a commitment to another human being? Or, is it a commitment to yourself where you *trust* that your belief claim is right? In the following section, we will continue our discussion on the ideas of knowledge, belief, and faith. In regards to the idea of *trust*, I will leave it up to each of you to decide for yourselves how you might think about trust. Remember that trust can take many forms: there are unlimited possibilities for how trust can make a difference in the world. With these possibilities in mind, let us move forward to Part II, *Scientific and Religious People*.

NOTE

1. Donald Wiebe, "The Ambiguous Revolution: Kant on the Nature of Faith," in *Beyond Legitimation: Essays on the Problem of Religious Knowledge* (New York: St. Martin's Press, Inc., 1994), 171.

II

Scientific and Religious People

Chapter Five

Religious Language

Do we have a religious epistemology (a religious *form of knowledge*)? Yes, probably, but the "language" of a religious epistemology is quite different from the "language" of a scientific epistemology. Previously we discussed scientific language—human expressions of scientific life. In this chapter we will consider religious language—human expressions of religious life. Sociologists Peter Berger and Thomas Luckmann are known for their theory of social construction where human beings create their own social worlds. A social world is how we interact with each other in a community—how we understand our place in relation to the rest of the world and to everyone else around us; how we understand "reality." Like any *theory*, Berger and Luckmann's theory is just that, a *theory*. Some people will agree with their theory while other people might disagree with their theory. Berger and Luckmann's theory is that the social world of a community was created by the community. (It might be a *knowledge community* composed of scientists or engineers or a *belief community* composed of religious or spiritual people.) The community members do not realize they created their own social world. Instead they believe their social world is something other than their own creation. Nevertheless the social world was in fact created by the community.[1] Berger and Luckmann explain some mechanisms[2] through which a social world is created, unknowingly, by a community: From birth, human beings are subject to various influences determined by the community in which they live. For one, languages help to create social worlds, providing human beings with the ability to separate their experiences into various knowledge categories. In a community, different roles are carried out by different individuals. Over time, these roles become routine, providing the community with an institutional framework (such as the framework of a school or a church). Also, the sharing of history between members of a community produces a body of knowledge passed from generation to generation. All of these factors contribute to the production of a social world in a community.

In his book *The Sacred Canopy: Elements of a Sociological Theory of Religion* (1967), Peter Berger observes, "Religion is the human enterprise by which a sacred cosmos is established,"[3] where *sacred* is "a quality of mysterious and awesome power, other than man [people] and yet related to him [them], which is believed to reside in certain objects of experience."[4] Here we have, yet again, another possible definition for the term *religion*. Berger's statement that religion is part of a "human enterprise"[5] and Berger and Luckmann's theory of social construction, are helpful to us as we seek a common ground in religious life—a level playing field where all of us, regardless of our own backgrounds and traditions, might come together to share our beliefs with one another. A common ground in religious life, where various beliefs are mixed, contrasts a position of absolute certainty in religion. Avoiding absolute certainty in religion is similar to avoiding the incorrect understanding in science that scientific theories are absolute truths. As Berger and another sociologist Anton Zijderveld explain, when a position of absolute certainty is taken in religion, a particular world view is formed where it is assumed that *all* questions of belief have already been answered and any suggestion of doubt in religion is frowned upon.[6] That is not a helpful view to take, especially when we are trying to understand the similarities and differences between the nature of scientific knowledge and the nature of religious belief. With religious language, we need space in our minds to adapt our beliefs were necessary; to learn about religion from our real life experiences of religion. These are the ideal human expressions of religion. If we are honest about our human condition, we know that we need to shape our religion by what we experience in life. Ultimately we would like to find a common ground among all knowledges and beliefs. Before the end of this adventure we may do just that.

At this point, I will introduce a new word to our adventure—a word that we have all probably heard and used at some point in our lives. The word is *theology*. I will suggest that *theology* might be telling stories about the gods, since the word *theology* is from the Classical Greek words *theos*—θεός—meaning *a god*, and *log*os—λόγος—which can mean *story*. (Note: The statement *the gods* is my simple way of pointing to a trans-empirical world without having to state *trans-empirical world* every time.) *Logos* also means *reason* or *rational*, so *theology* might also be providing a reason for the gods or a rational account of the gods. It is interesting that the term *rational* is coming up again, but this time it is arising from the Greek word *logos*. As we have already seen with our attempts to define the words *science* and *religion*, coming up with simple definitions for any of these words (and now we have the word *theology* to consider) is really not possible. Instead these words have various definitions, which might all be right in various contexts or we have to pick the definitions that we ourselves prefer. It is also important that we consider a difference between the terms *religion* and *theology*, because these terms are thought, by some philosophers of religion, to be not so interchangeable. Sound intriguing? Read on. . . .

Assuming that each religion possesses its own mythological integrity and if the origins of religions are rooted in mythological narratives, then to be a person who thinks religiously is to be a person who thinks within a world view where meaning is derived from the mythological integrity of the person's religion. Mythological narratives tell stories of superhuman agents who cause events to occur in the world. With this understanding of religious thinking in mind, it is not difficult to see why there are so many different religious traditions in the world. Each religion developed from its own mythological narratives and each tradition tells a story of a different superhuman agent. Given my use of the term *mythological* here, as it relates to religion, I must say that if a narrative (story) is mythological that doesn't necessarily mean the narrative does not express truth. Our human minds can be oriented by myths so that the myths, which are often based on symbols and metaphors, provide us with meaning and purpose in our lives. Myths serve a function that is connected to our need as human beings to experience belief about a trans-empirical world. Our human thoughts, emotions, hopes, and fears, are all given a meaningful context when they relate to myths. Myths are not the same as fairy tales. Myths are images which create a *form* of religious knowledge. Within the images of myths, we, as human beings, come to understand what it means to *think religiously*. Another way to say this is that myths are the epistemology of religion—myths are the *form of knowledge* of religion. Myths also "speak" with the character of a religious authority.

Donald Wiebe suggests we might view *theology* as our attempt to place this aspect of the world, where myths and superhuman agents are the primary modes of thinking, into a knowledge framework that is more similar to the knowledge framework (epistemology) of science.[7] This allows us to approach the subject of the gods in a rational way (learning from experience) that avoids the use of a mythological narrative. As Wiebe outlines, this type of theology may be described as "talk about God" theology, which suggests a rational study of religious thinking. "Talk about God" theology is contrasted to "God-talk" theology, which suggests a study of religious thinking within a mythological world view.[8] "God-talk" theology is not always tolerated in the West, because it depends on a mythological world view that we all cannot agree on. From this point onward, I won't focus anymore on definitions for the terms *science*, *religion*, or *theology*. We now possess enough fodder for these words to carry us through to the end of our adventure. It is important though that we keep in mind everything we have read so far about these complex and eclectic words. If you want to take one thing away from reading this book, it is that if anyone ever tells you what any of these words mean, and that their definitions are the most "correct" definitions, you turn and run the other way! There is never a most "correct" definition for any of these words. An important part of being an adjudicator is understanding that and being *open* to alternative definitions as they are presented.

NOTES

1. Peter L. Berger and Thomas Luckmann, *The Social Construction of Reality* (New York: Anchor Books, 1966), 61.
2. Berger and Luckmann, *The Social Construction of Reality*, 47ff.
3. Peter L. Berger, *The Sacred Canopy: Elements of a Sociological Theory of Religion* (New York: Anchor Books, 1967), 25.
4. Berger, *The Sacred Canopy*, 25.
5. Ibid.
6. Peter L. Berger and Anton C. Zijderveld, *In Praise of Doubt: How to Have Convictions Without Becoming a Fanatic* (New York: HarperCollins, 2009), 158.
7. Donald Wiebe, *The Irony of Theology and the Nature of Religious Thought* (Montreal: McGill-Queen's University Press, 1991), 12.
8. Wiebe, *The Irony of Theology and the Nature of Religious Thought*, 15.

Chapter Six

Some Unexpected Surprises

Most contrasts and comparisons of science and religion are centered on differences or similarities between scientific and religious modes of thought. This, of course, has always opened up a wide range of possibilities for how one might go about contrasting or comparing science and religion (and inevitably very little agreement on whether science and religion are different or similar). As we've begun to see, for an adjudicator, who "measures" the acceptability or legitimacy of human knowledges and beliefs, this "measuring" work depends upon each adjudicator's own assumptions, biases, and life experiences. An adjudicator's life experience is important—our *experience* is often the one thing that separates our lives from everyone else's lives, providing us with a unique perspective that we own and can share. Recently, in the 21st century, a new approach to contrasting and comparing science and religion was developed by scholars. These scholars, who include a mix of philosophers of science, experimental psychologists, and anthropologists, have been looking at whether science and religion might be understood through the systems of *cognitive science*. Again, as in all work surrounding science and religion, whether or not an adjudicator brings a faith position into the mix is a personal decision. (We have already considered the implications of this, and will continue to do so, but I just wanted to remind you of how the option of utilizing a faith position, or not, is a personal decision, left up to each individual adjudicator.)

Philosopher of science Robert N. McCauley in his interesting book *Why Religion Is Natural and Science Is Not* (2011) explains to us how, although philosophical approaches are utilized to explain scientific or religious exercises, a comparison of science and religion using the systems of cognitive science is also possible.[1] In general terms, cognitive science is a field of research which studies the activity of the human mind, focusing on the ability of the human mind to receive information through perception, to process information in thoughts, and to utilize information by actions. The conclusions reached by a study of "science and religion" using cognitive science present us with some unexpected surprises, as suggested by the title of McCauley's book *Why Religion Is Natural and Science Is Not*. Somehow it may be easier to be a religious person (natural activity) than it is to be a scientific person (unnatural activity). I have included this chapter to help us become aware of this different approach to science and religion, where the internal systems of the human mind are the focus. As adjudicators, we obviously use our minds to help us measure knowledge or belief claims, so it seems important that we also learn a bit about what is going on *inside* our own human minds. I really have no control over the systems of my human mind any more than I have control over how my lunch is digested in my stomach! To talk about "systems" of the human mind may be a bit misleading (a "system" might imply some kind of physical structure), but a "system" can also refer to a pattern of thoughts or the order of steps that are taken to make sense of new information—these systems are the "systems" of the human mind.

McCauley's thesis is that religious thinking develops in our human minds from a *natural* cognitive system—a system of thinking we were born with. Interestingly, like religion, the activity of *technology* (distinct from the activity of science) is also a natural human activity. Although it may seem counterintuitive, McCauley suggests that scientific exercises are different. The system of thinking utilized in scientific exercises is a system of *reflection*—a system of thinking we were not born with, but a system we had to learn. So, science is *unnatural*. This doesn't mean that science doesn't have a purpose (indeed we have seen how science very much has a purpose, providing us with tested and useful knowledge), but what this means is that scientific thinking, which allows us to propose ideas, test them, and then keep those ideas or throw them away, is an *unnatural* activity. We have to learn or discover how to complete the work of science. Apparently, we don't have to learn or discover religion. Instead, a capacity for "religion" is already there in our minds. At this point, we must separate the terms *religion* (a term we've been using throughout this book) and the term *religiosity*. While it may be the case that a capacity for "religion" is already there in our minds, we don't want to imply that the cultural trappings of religion are already there. The point here is not that religious institutions, rituals, or religious texts develop naturally inside our minds (in fact, we saw in the previous chapter how those things are created in the context of a social world). The point here is that *religious thinking* or *religiosity* develop naturally in our minds.

What exactly is *religiosity*? Well, I think we answered that question previously when we discussed our need as human beings to possess beliefs about trans-empirical worlds or beliefs about gods. Religiosity and religious thinking are about searching for (and possibly identifying) a god or gods. Religiosity and religious thinking are also about using a god or gods to explain our human existence on earth. However, just because we learn, through cognitive science, how we possess a natural desire to search for a god or gods, that doesn't mean that a god or gods exist. What it means is that we possess a natural desire to search for a god or gods. (That distinction is important.) To play "devil's advocate" for a moment, is it possible that, in our natural desire to search for a god or gods (part of our natural religiosity), we are actually searching for something else—something from our evolutionary heritage—which today we interpret to be a god or gods? Some researchers in cognitive science, who study the phenomenon of religious thinking, are prepared to say that, yes, our desire to search for "something" (call it a "god" or call it something else) is part of our evolutionary heritage, linked directly to our need to survive. In fact, the desire to search for "something" has a very specific evolutionary purpose. Some religious people now use a faith position, going one step further to suggest that the god who looks after them in their religious tradition has "set up" evolution in this way, making sure that human beings have a need to search for "something." That search, they argue, led people to discover the real life existence of the god. This is an example of how a faith position can voluntarily be used to "tweak" the outcome of scientific work. However, in the next paragraph, let me provide you with the official scientific description (without a faith position) of humans searching for "something" and how this searching is connected with our evolutionary past:

Pretend for a moment you are living about 100,000 years ago when our species of human, *Homo sapiens*, began to exist in a way anatomically similar to us today. (To give you some context, the universe began some 13.8 billion years ago, so to pretend you are living about 100,000 years ago is not really to go back that far!) With the possibility of predators (e.g. panthers) nearby, you are going to need some way to detect the presence of predators. You need a way to identify predators, so that you have time to make the necessary arrangements and get away. Further still, predators are very good at sneaking up behind you, watching you from a distance, and then making their attack when you are least expecting it. So, it is extremely important that you are extra vigilant. Your survival depends on it! Thankfully, the processes of natural selection in evolutionary biology, which you inherited from your ancestors, did you a favor. Your ancestors survived only because they were good at detecting the presence of predators, allowing them time to get away before predators attacked. It is also the case that your ancestors had some friends who were not so good at detecting the presence of predators—those people did not survive very long in this perilous world. The people who survived, because they were good at detecting the presence of predators, unknowingly passed on to you a cognitive system from inside their own human minds. You now benefit from this cognitive system, which keeps you extra vigilant, allowing you to detect the presence of predators and survive.

Sometimes you might think there are predators watching you, but actually there are none. This is called a false-positive, because you thought there were predators when actually there weren't. However, to your advantage, your mind has been conditioned in a certain way (by evolution) to always assume there might be predators, so that, when there actually are predators, you have time to get away and survive. It would be much worse if you weren't extra vigilant and then predators that are watching you (which you didn't know about) end up attacking. That is called a false-negative, because you didn't think there were predators, when actually there were. So long as the effects of detecting false-positives are not too damaging to your human psyche (perhaps detecting false-positives result only in overly cautious or anxious human beings), a natural desire to detect the presence of "something" is useful. As McCauley interestingly observes, ". . . the creature that is inattentive to the movement in the periphery, the shadow passing overhead, or the rustling in the leaves (let alone the sound in the basement) is less prepared to protect itself from predators, competitors, and foes."[2] Eventually, as civilizations developed (about 5,000 years ago) and human beings began to live in larger communities separated from predators, the need to detect the presence of predators became less important. Today our human minds still contain "fossil" remnants of our natural desire to detect predators or to detect "something." We just can't help ourselves. How many times have you woken up in the night, heard "something," and your natural response was to assume danger (even though there was no obvious reason to really think danger)? If you have ever gone on a camping trip, deep in the woods, you'll know exactly what I mean!

For our early human ancestors, the activity of technology included the making of tools, artifacts, and clothing. Technology has certainly functioned as a catalyst in the growth of scientific knowledge; however, science, as one human activity, is different from technology, another human activity. For one, technology, a natural activity that does not require reflective thought patterns, can exist without the invention of writing and without the development of literacy. Science, an unnatural activity that is reflective (because you have to test your own knowledge claims and question your own beliefs), requires the skills of reading and writing to be able to function effectively. Historians of technology have suggested that up until the end of the 19th century the development of technology was unrelated to science.[3] Technology was based on a human phenomenon (capacity) of its own. Natural history also testifies to this as we observe evidence of tool making in species other than our own. Archaeologist Steven Mithen's theory of cognitive fluidity explains the transference of information between various mental modules (systems) within the human mind. Cognitive fluidity may be helpful in explaining the development of rationality and science. It may be that separate mental modules, where information in the mind is strictly encapsulated in individual modules, represents the mind prior to the evolution of cognitive fluidity. Prior to the evolution of cognitive fluidity, the activities of technology and religiosity (detecting "something") were already possible—each activity originated from within its own mental module (e.g. modules accounting for information from material or social worlds). In contrast, it appears the existence of science depended upon the evolution of cognitive fluidity where information is transferred between different mental modules, allowing for reflective activity. As mentioned, science is a reflective activity, because you need to be reflective of your own work to be able to test your knowledge claims and you cannot just take things for granted. Perhaps this rules out the possibility that our very, very early human ancestors (100,000 years ago) participated in scientific activity. Still, we cannot ever really know. What has been called into question is whether the human mind was always uniform? Or, has the human mind existed at different times with different mental systems and therefore with different capacities for thought? Yes, that does seem to be the case. Read on. . . .

In the 19th and 20th centuries, attempts were made to classify "ancient" and "modern" human minds into various categories—"primitive versus advanced," "wild versus domesticated," "mythological versus empirical," or "closed versus open"—and to study the differences between these human minds as outcomes of our evolutionary past. However, anthropologists questioned whether these categories are really fair? After all, as modern humans, we are studying the ancient human mind from the perspective of our own modern world view (which includes the benefits of science). Therefore, is it really fair to call the ancient human mind "primitive" or "wild" and then turn around and call our modern human mind "advanced" or "domesticated"? (In academic terms, this is called an ethnocentric bias.) A different school of thought prefers to utilize a kind of cultural relativism—to assume that all people, in the history of the human species, are equal. This approach discourages the idea of comparing "our" society (modern) to "their" society (ancient). However, what do we do if it does seem that, from an evolutionary perspective, the human mind was functioning differently 100,000 years ago or even just, say, 30,000 years ago? Well, it is okay to acknowledge this and, as we've seen, these differences may shed some light on why science did or did not exist in very early times. (Later on in our adventure, we will in fact see that something like modern science was happening about 2,500 years ago.) As long as we are not pointing our fingers, and saying "our" society knows more about the world than "their" society did, I think we are being fair. Yes, we might say that our modern human minds have a greater capacity to acquire knowledge (and adjudicate knowledge) than ancient human minds did. However, in the context that ancient humans lived, their own ancient human minds served them just fine. Also, we can't ever be sure that one day future humans will look back on us and think, wow, those people who lived in the 21st century really didn't get it! They were the "ancient" ones!

Let me take one paragraph, then, to commit the sin of having an ethnocentric bias. This way you can at least see how, from our perspective, the ancient human mind could be different from the modern human mind. In this paragraph, I am going to assume that my modern mind gives me something the ancient mind just didn't have (this is my ethnocentric bias). I am going to assume that, unlike the ancient mind, my modern mind makes use of modern science and scientific thinking. French anthropologist Lucien Lévy-Bruhl (b. 1857, d. 1939) called the ancient mind "pre-logical" and the modern mind "logical." Pre-logical thinking implies some kind of mythological thinking (in contrast from logical or empirical thinking, which is based on tested knowledge claims). In mythological thinking, a person never asks, "how did something happen?" Rather, in mythological thinking, a person asks, "*who caused something to happen?*"[4] From our modern perspective, it appears that many of our earliest human ancestors lived in a so-called mythological world. When a tree in the forest fell down, our ancestors did not ask, "*how did the tree fall down?*" The question "how did the tree fall down?" expects an answer based on empirical science, such as the force of hanging branches on one side of the tree was greater than the force of branches on the other side, and so the tree fell down in the direction of the greater force. Instead, when a tree in the forest fell down, our prehistoric ancestors asked, "*who caused the tree to fall down?*" The question "who caused the tree to fall down?" expects an answer based on myth, such as the god of the forest was angry that we were trespassing in the forest and so the god of the forest made the tree fall down, in an attempt to hit us. This focus on "who" (rather than "how") may be related to the idea of searching for the presence of "something" in the world. Searching for the presence of "something" may be an evolutionary outcome from when the earliest humans were detecting the presence of predators, especially in a hyper-vigilant state. Whatever the case, the thinking that goes on in the ancient mind takes place in the context of a dynamic relationship with the natural world. For the ancient mind, the natural world, external to you or me, is "alive" and changing—not changing because of mechanical forces, chemical reactions, or evolutionary biology, but changing because the natural world is full of gods. These gods cause events to occur in the world. In contrast, as a modern human being with a modern mind, I do not see the external world as being "alive," but rather I understand causes of events using scientific theories. These causes might involve mechanical forces, chemical reactions, or evolutionary biology. In a later chapter, called *Causes and Explanatory Forces*, we will revisit some of these ideas. For now, remember the important distinction between "how" questions (scientific thinking) and "who" questions (mythological thinking).

NOTES

1. Robert N. McCauley, *Why Religion Is Natural and Science Is Not* (New York: Oxford University Press, 2011), 3.
2. McCauley, *Why Religion Is Natural and Science Is Not*, 82.
3. Ibid., 91.
4. H. A. Frankfort and Henri Frankfort, "Myth and Reality," in *The Intellectual Adventure of Ancient Man: An Essay on Speculative Thought in the Ancient Near East* (Chicago: The University of Chicago Press, 1946), 15.

Chapter Seven

Faces of Religion / Faces of Science

The strange dichotomy between religious fellowships and secular life—the strange tension between theological faith and scientific reason—has interestingly not prevented us from bringing our faiths into the 21st century where the standards of probable reasoning stand as the measuring bars for deciding what knowledge is. It appears that a tension between theological faith and scientific reason has existed before. One famous example is from Oxford, England, in 1860. Samuel Wilberforce, the Anglican bishop of Oxford, participated in a debate with Thomas Huxley, a biologist and supporter of the theory of evolution. This was a struggle for religion in the face of science or, as some might want to phrase it, a struggle for science in the face of religion. Wilberforce argued for a biblical account of the creation of the world whereas Huxley argued for evolution by natural selection. At the end of the debate, it was not clear which side of the debate had actually won, but rather it seems that both sides went away feeling like winners.[1] Debates surrounding a compatibility system between science and religion continue to this day without any clear method for adjudicating which side has won. Donald Wiebe in his essay *Science and Religion: Is Compatibility Possible?* (1978, republished 1994) defines a compatibility system as follows: "A compatibility system of thought is essentially a justification of accepting two apparently conflicting systems of thought. If no *prima facie* conflict [conflict based on a first impression] existed, there would be no impetus to construct such a system."[2] For most people, upon first impression, science and religion are in conflict, encompassing two separate domains of reality with distinct "languages" and distinct methods. Some point out that these separate domains of reality are best distinguished by the difference between "how" questions (the realm of science/knowledge) and "why" (or "who") questions (the realm of religion/belief). A "how" question states *how is there something rather than nothing?*

In this case, we expect to hear a mechanistic explanation for a phenomenon in the natural world. In contrast, a "why" question states *why is there something rather than nothing?* In this case, we expect to hear an answer concerning human meaning and purpose. The distinction between "how" and "why" questions is helpful, but let us take science out of the picture briefly and see how we also categorize various religious identities as being different from one another.

While I studied for my master's degree in theological studies, I worked as a school chaplain in a high school and as a preacher in a small town church in Ontario, Canada. In both roles, I found that people expressed various types of faiths even if they all identified with the same religion. You might have experienced something similar. Or, if you haven't, you can probably appreciate that religious diversity (even within a single religion) is inevitable. Think of all the possible definitions that we came up with for the word *religion*. Then consider that different people will probably focus on different definitions for the word *religion*. The expressions of different people's faiths are going to vary for sure. To illustrate this point, we might consider that faiths in Judaism are expressed in various forms which differ in their interpretations of Mosaic Law and in the cultural trappings they possess. There are also non-religious Jews, living in Tel Aviv, who cease from work on Saturday to observe a religious law (*Shabbat*), suggesting some faith expression also for secular Jews. In my work with middle school and teenaged students, I met kids who said they believed different things: Some students said they believe in a god. Those students were from different religions, so some said they believe in God while others said they believe in Allah. Other students said they did not believe in a god. It is wise to be cautious of how we label others (of any age) who say they do not believe in God, Allah, or another superhuman agent. Who knows what any one of us really thinks? Can a single word really ever describe the intricacies of our innermost thoughts, especially our religious thoughts? The word *atheist* tends to be used quite loosely in different ways by different people. For some, it may simply be the best way to describe their disinterest in organized religions (institutions). For others, it may be a cool fad amongst friends to appear as one who is anti-religious and using the term *atheist* is the best way to make that point. The real faiths of people who say they do not believe in a god may indicate situations quite different! Likewise the real faiths of people who say they believe in a god may not be quite what we expected either! (There are a lot of different people with a lot of different belief systems; they all use the term *theist*.) I also met students who were interested in having a faith, but were unsure of how to go about developing a faith. (Here I say *having a faith* rather than *having faith* to emphasize the point that expression of one person's faith is never the same as expression of another person's faith—multiple people, even if all from a single religion, express multiple *faiths*, not *faith*.) For a person who is exploring the life of a faith, religious narratives provide a spiritual framework that is relevant to one's life. Religious narratives tell us about our religion by relating religion to our everyday lives. From your own religious tradition, choose a particular story from your religion's text. Perhaps reflect on how that religious story influenced your life in the past and how that story influences your life in the present.

In the preceding paragraph, I used the terms *atheist* and *theist*. In popular culture *theist* is used to label a person who says he or she believes in God. In contrast *atheist* is used to label a person who says he or she does not believe in God. (As in earlier sections, in these examples, I am using the term *God*, but *Allah* or the name of another mythological superhuman agent—*Zeus*, *Attis*, *Adonis*, etc.—could be substituted here.) The problem with the terms *atheist* and *theist* is that these terms, however useful they may be to categorize groups of people, are only labels. A single label cannot adequately describe a person's religious beliefs or the factors in one's life that led to those particular beliefs. Some people's beliefs change throughout their lives (we eliminate some beliefs and/or add other beliefs to our conscious minds), but people retain the meaning or purpose in life that arose from previous beliefs even if those beliefs are based on religious stories now understood to be historically irrelevant. An analogy to this problem of labels is to consider the suitability of words used to describe a person's genetic sexual orientation, such as the words *gay* or *straight*. These words are helpful, but if used strictly to label people they become problematic—contemporary expressions of sexuality are far more diverse than anything that a single label can describe. There is a similar problem with the words *atheist* or *theist*. These words are helpful, and a lot of people willingly choose to identify with them, but once they become labels from which no other thinking is possible they become restricting. Another term, commonly used by some, is Thomas Huxley's term *agnostic*, which describes a person who says there is no way to know whether or not God exists. (Thomas Huxley was the biologist mentioned earlier who participated in a famous debate about science and religion in 1860.) Another term, although much less commonly used, is *igtheist* coined by philosopher Paul Kurtz (b. 1925, d. 2012) in his book *The New Skepticism: Inquiry and Reliable Knowledge* (1992). An *igtheist* is a person who says that the statement *God exists* is a meaningless statement.[3] *Ig* represents the term *ignorant*, so an *igtheist* is ignorant of God, but *igtheist* is not meant to be a negative word. Instead, an *igtheist* makes the point that if we cannot agree on a definition for "God" or if we cannot agree on what or who "God" is, then how can we possibly expect to discuss whether or not "God" exists? Kurtz explains the life of an igtheist as follows: "I cannot say whether or not such a being [God] exists since I do not comprehend what is being asserted."[4] It is an attractive label, I must say, even for a person like me who dislikes religious labels in general. At any rate, now moving ahead in our adventure, we have four different terms to pick from (if we choose to pick): i) *atheist*, ii) *theist*, iii) *agnostic*, or iv) *igtheist*. Take your pick, but remember these words are only starting points. They shouldn't prevent us from expanding our thinking beyond their simple definitions.

A comment on *faith* itself—yet again another word in the vocabulary of our adventure! I won't offer a definition per se for the word *faith* (I said before that we are finished dwelling on definitions), but there is an interesting Hebrew use of *faith* I will discuss in this chapter. Religious people have often understood faith to include a belief of "God" and a trust in "God." Rendered in the Greek, faith is *pistis*—πίστις—a concept that includes belief and trust. The ancient Hebrew word *aman*—אמן—a verb, means *confirm*. Here is an ancient grammar lesson: In ancient Hebrew, the Hiphil verbal stem is a verbal stem which is used to convey a verbal meaning that causes a condition to come into being.[5] So, the Hiphil verbal construction of *aman* would mean *cause to confirm* (the condition that comes into being is a condition of *confirmation*). Other English translations for the Hiphil verbal form of *aman* are *believe* and *trust*,[6] which are the components of faith. For example, the following passage from Genesis in the Torah uses a Hiphil verbal form of *aman* and translates that form into English as *believe*: "They told him, 'Joseph is still alive! In fact, he is ruler of all Egypt.' Jacob was stunned; he did not *believe* them."[7] When we speak about faith in general we usually presuppose (assume) that God exists. In fact, when speaking about a trans-empirical world, some religious people will use faith as the explanation for why they are convinced that God exists. They will say something along the lines of: "I know through faith (belief and trust) that God exists." This is all well and good (and sounds meaningful when going to, say, funerals), but I would like us to consider whether this is an appropriate assumption for an adjudicator to make? Should we assume that the action of faith *is* the powerful force that religious people make it out to be? If we desire to act as neutral, dispassionate, and unbiased observers of religion—people who evaluate the merits of religion from "outside" of religion—we also have to be prepared to evaluate the merits of the assumptions made by ourselves and other religious people (and other scientific people). We make assumptions every day whether we realize it or not. Assumptions can radically change the ways in which we pursue and evaluate knowledge claims in religion and in science. Don't jump too quickly, because I not saying you should drop the assumption that God exists; however, you do need to become aware of that assumption. Also, if your assumption is that God does not exist, I am not suggesting you drop that assumption either, but rather become aware of it.

Throughout this book, I've been mentioning the idea of modern Western research or modern science especially in a Western context. I have done this, because I was a student in a North American country and most of the experience I bring to this book arose from a Western context. However, I don't mean at all to imply that modern science doesn't exist in other parts of the world. For example, during the Middle Ages, it was Baghdad that was the intellectual centre of the world. While the small-minded people in Europe were busy burning witches and disemboweling heretics, Baghdad was thriving and, from what we know, a very scientific place! This chapter is called *Faces of Religion / Faces of Science*. We already considered "faces of religion" when we discussed how various people, even if all from a single religion, express their faiths in various ways. For "faces of science," I'd like us to consider (briefly) how scientific work is not always expressed or understood in the same way by different scientists or engineers. We learned how it is important to understand that scientific knowledge is not about truths, but scientific knowledge is about scientific theories. At this point I have to confess that there are a lot of scientists and engineers who would not agree with me, at all! That is okay, because in writing this book I am functioning as a student of the philosophy of science (so, as your leader in this adventure, I can say things about science that real life scientists or engineers may not agree with). The fact is there is probably a mix of scientists and engineers out there in the world—some who think that science is about theories and others who are sure that science is about the absolute truth. In the same way, there is probably a mix of religious and spiritual people out there in the world—some who think that religion is about a way of life, which can evolve and change, and others who are sure that religion is about the absolute truth. Think of the absolute truth as "the truth, the whole truth, and nothing but the truth." Within the absolute truth, there is no room for any change; no room for us to tweak our knowledges and beliefs in the future. I just don't know if either science or religion can give us something like the absolute truth. I don't think we can pretend that knowledges and beliefs are never going to evolve and change in the future. In the past they certainly did change. They likely will continue to do so.

Let me provide you with an example from science where science does not seem to be about the absolute truth: In quantum physics (one of the most advanced forms of physics which has existed since the 20th century), it is not possible to determine the exact location of an electron, a subatomic particle, located inside an atom. What happens is that when we attempt to observe an electron, using our scientific apparatus, we end up forcing the electron to choose a particular place to be located. Our very act of being experimental observers forces the electron to make a choice—does it want to be "here" or does it want to be "there"? This is all well and good, because in using our scientific apparatus we get to "see" the electron, but we can't ever know where the electron was originally located! There is also the possibility we have imagined the idea of electrons and just thought that we "saw" them. Perhaps in trying to observe a so-called "electron," and figure out where it is located, what is actually happening is we are creating the *idea* of an electron.

Who knows? Maybe electrons or atoms don't even physically exist: perhaps they serve as useful models to *visualize* physical reality, but they are really ideas in our imaginations! (Perhaps the gods are that way too!) Here, the important point to take home with you is that science can, at times, be vague. It's possible that some physicists will dislike my description about the "vagueness" of electrons, because I deliberately pointed out how, when acting as experimental observers and performing an experiment, we influence the thing (electron) being observed. In response, some physicists might say something to the effect that, "with electrons, we are doing the best that we can do for the time being." I would be okay with that kind of response. Science is about coming up with the best theories or models we have for the time being. In the future, science may improve. (It likely will.) We just have to be careful that we always remember that and also that we never let science rule over us; that we never let science have the "final say."

The faces of religion and the faces of science rarely, if ever, coalesce well with each other. It is as if religion and science were two human beings who spoke different languages. Each knows the other exists, each can see the other, and each wishes to speak with the other. But, they just can't communicate. The barrier of speaking different languages makes communication impossible. That being said, we, as people who utilize the faces of religion and the faces of science in our personal lives, seem able to overcome this barrier. If we want to, we seem able to reconcile differences between religion and science. It's not always clear how we do that. Science is always questioning things—looking for other options, keeping itself open to change, and transforming society. Religion, in its most traditional sense, just doesn't seem to want to do that. (In its own way, certain aspects of religion, for example, a belief about a god who protects us, can transform society; however, that transformation is a very different type of transformation from the transformation of science. The transformation of science is based on tested knowledge; the transformation of religion is not.) So, ultimately, a conflict between religion and science is inevitable. I'm not saying which one is right or wrong (religion *or* science), but it seems a conflict cannot be avoided. It may be that most of us are aware of this conflict, but we really just don't think it matters. Perhaps we deny there is a conflict. Some of us might trust that, somehow, the world will figure itself out.

In the past, various cultures were aware of the problem of trying to reconcile religion with science or religion with any kind of natural knowledge. Turkish Arabic was the language of the Ottoman Empire, which lasted for a striking seven centuries, from 1299 until the First World War. In Turkish Arabic, there are two words for *knowledge*. The first word is *ilm* which is knowledge of natural things and also knowledge of religious matters. Scientists in the Ottoman Empire realized this might be a problem. They understood that scientific knowledge (knowledge of natural things) was quite different from knowledge of religious matters. So, they created a second word for knowledge, *fen*, which is exclusively knowledge of tools or techniques.[8] They used *fen* to describe knowledge of natural things and then *ilm* was left for knowledge of religious matters. It seems this Ottoman convention didn't really catch on, and today the word *ilm* is used for most types of knowledges, scientific and religious, in the Arabic-speaking world. Nevertheless, we see how, for the Ottomans, problems about how to distinguish different types of knowledges (natural and religious) were relevant. Much earlier, in the first few centuries, Tertullian, sometimes called the founder of Western theology, remarked, "What has Athens to do with Jerusalem?" His remark was a direct reference to the fact that people in Athens were concerned with knowledge of the natural world whereas people in Jerusalem had a different purpose, which was to study knowledge of religious matters. It seems Tertullian was one person who didn't want to see these separate domains of knowledge (natural and religious) getting mixed up. Still, more recently in the 20th century, others were looking for ways to get religion and science to somehow coalesce and join together. In 1951 the religious leader of the Roman Catholic Church, Pope Pius XII, declared that the Big Bang theory does not conflict with the biblical account of creation found in the Book of Genesis. (He also seemed to suggest that the Big Bang might even be "evidence" for a Creator.[9]) In another story, the Higgs boson, a very small particle which is important in understanding much of physical reality, has been nicknamed, by some, the "God particle." However, researchers working on the Higgs boson in Switzerland have remarked that the nickname "God particle" is not really an appropriate term for the Higgs boson.

So, the problem of dealing with a conflict between religion and science is not new: it's been around for a long time and will probably continue to be around in the future. In our adventure, we are learning about a special way to deal with this conflict, which is by understanding how to work as adjudicators. We learn how to decide, for ourselves, which knowledges and beliefs count as legitimate knowledges and beliefs. We are each becoming our own adjudicators. We function as adjudicators using the philosophical and theological tools we have been learning about. (I will summarize these tools later.) As adjudicators, assumptions we make about the world are very important. As mentioned, we need to become aware of our assumptions (some of which may have been hanging around in the backs of our minds since we were children). We become good adjudicators only after we analyze our own thinking down to the assumptions that we make. For example, is it right to make the assumption that a trans-empirical world possesses a reality beyond the visible world? As my professor Donald Wiebe observes, this type of dilemma amounts to the question of whether the activity of "thinking about the gods,"[10] a phrase including various types of religious modes of thought, is to be accomplished with or without an assumption about the *nature* of the gods?

We can ask ourselves the following questions: Do the gods have being or do the gods not have being? Does a trans-empirical world exist independent of this world or is a trans-empirical world a product of a socially constructed reality? Using Berger and Luckmann's terminology for the creation of social worlds (discussed previously), have we *created* the idea of a trans-empirical world in our imaginations? Do we now experience the effects of a trans-empirical world as something other than our own creation? Or, as some people might ask, is the idea of social construction flawed, because social construction is actually a circular argument? I will consider this last question and explain *circular argument* in the next chapter.

NOTES

1. Philip Luscombe, *Groundwork of Science and Religion* (Peterborough: Epworth Press, 2000), 2.
2. Donald Wiebe, "Science and Religion: Is Compatibility Possible?" in *Beyond Legitimation: Essays on the Problem of Religious Knowledge* (New York: St. Martin's Press, Inc., 1994), 58.
3. Paul Kurtz, *The New Skepticism: Inquiry and Reliable Knowledge* (Buffalo: Prometheus Books, 1992), 197.
4. Kurtz, *The New Skepticism*, 197.
5. Choon-Leong Seow, *A Grammar for Biblical Hebrew* (Nashville: Abingdon Press, 1995), 181.
6. Seow, *A Grammar for Biblical Hebrew*, 221.
7. Gen. 45:26 (New International Version).
8. Ehsan Masood, *Science and Islam: A History* (London: Icon Books Ltd, 2009), xi.
9. Lawrence M. Krauss, *A Universe from Nothing: Why There Is Something Rather Than Nothing* (New York: Free Press, 2012), 4.
10. Donald Wiebe, *The Irony of Theology and the Nature of Religious Thought* (Montreal: McGill-Queen's University Press, 1991), 10.

Chapter Eight

Knowledge and Belief Communities

Our philosopher of science, Thomas Kuhn, and his use of *paradigms* is going to be helpful here. In *The Structure of Scientific Revolutions*, Kuhn described some methods through which scientific research is accomplished.[1] I summarize these methods as follows:

1. A first method is that facts, known through previous research, are applied to solve scientific problems. These facts may be any of the following: numerical constants (e.g. Planck's constant, a fundamental physical constant, which is 6.63×10^{-34} m² kg/s, a very, very small number), formulas (e.g. Newton's second law that force is mass multiplied by acceleration, expressed as the formula $F=ma$), or other laws (e.g. the second law of thermodynamics which says that the disorder of an isolated system will always become more disordered).
2. A second method is to apply the theories of a paradigm to solve a real life problem. For example, applying the theories of, say, electrochemistry to solve a chemical engineering problem.
3. A final method, and Kuhn believes this method to be the most common method in scientific research,[2] is to work on resolving ambiguities in a scientific theory which helps to make the theory stronger and more reliable.

When we read modern scientific texts or classical scientific works, such as Sir Isaac Newton's famous *Philosophiae Naturalis Principia Mathematica* (*Mathematical Principles of Natural Philosophy*, 1687), we read about scientific achievements that provided a *foundation* for new scientific research.[3] We also read about new theories that replaced old theories. All of this information makes up the content of the history of science. An understanding of the history of science is helpful to realize how scientific theories came to exist while also realizing that new theories are necessary to keep science progressing (recall that even Newton was aware that in the future science would improve). Without an awareness of the history of science, the work of science can become suspicious of new theories, because we forget that it is okay for new theories to come along. A lot of existing (old) theories are good theories, so they are here to stay, but we need to be *open* to the possibility of new theories. From Kuhn's philosophy, one of the most important things we learn is that our Western culture may see the work of "normal science," as the work, not of formulating new theories, but of expressing and then re-expressing older theories that already exist.[4] However, this type of science is limiting and not very creative. We may have failed to realize that even paradigms, which provide a foundation for future research, were once composed of new theories themselves and were not based on a foundation of previous research.

In *The Structure of Scientific Revolutions*, Thomas Kuhn makes the startling point that if science is never willing to abandon an old paradigm, science will never progress to better and brighter things—this is why his book was controversial when it was published in 1962, because he called into question the value of real life work done by scientists and engineers.[5] A "revolution" in science is a chance for a new paradigm to be developed, referred to by Kuhn as "extraordinary science"[6] (in contrast to "normal science"). Now, to recap a few things: Through our discussion of paradigms we begin to see that knowledge claims in science carry with them a long history of previous research. In fact, a knowledge claim in science is accepted only if it adheres to the foundation of research within a particular paradigm. At this point in our adventure we are led to the following question: has science become too focused on a way of thinking where the old theories of a paradigm determine *all* future scientific study? If this is indeed the case (or usually the case), and any new theory is viewed as unacceptable, then it appears that science as we know it may not be as open-minded and creative as we would like to think. Similar to a religious world view where it is assumed that all questions of belief have already been answered and any suggestion of doubt in religion is frowned upon, a scientific world view becomes limiting when there is no opportunity to develop a new theory and any suggestion of doubt in a current scientific theory is viewed as unacceptable.

We will now begin to see a connection between scientific knowledge claims and religious knowledge claims. It is my aim to show that, similar to disagreements in theology over which religion is the most "correct" religion, there can be disagreements in science about which theory is the most "correct" theory. Competing scientific theories are faced with the same problem as competing religions: we do not possess any supra-scientific framework or supra-theological framework that we can use to adjudicate which scientific theory or which religion is the most "correct." Here is a summary of this important epiphany: In science, the decision of whether one group's theory is more valid than another's will be based on each scientific group using its own theory to justify itself. In theology, the decision of whether one group's religion is more valid than another's will be based on each religious group using its own religion to justify itself. In both cases, the defenses of the most "correct" theory or the most "correct" religion are circular arguments, because each group is "trapped" inside the world view of its own theory or religion. The arguments each group uses for the defense of the most "correct" theory or most "correct" religion arise from within the world views of each group.

In this chapter we speak about the idea of a knowledge community composed of scientists or engineers. A knowledge community might exist in a university department, a place of modern research, or within an engineering company. We also speak about the idea of a belief community composed of religious or spiritual people. A belief community might exist in a church or in a place where spiritual people gather together. In applying Peter Berger and Thomas Luckmann's theory of social construction to a *knowledge community*, we observe that a knowledge community working under a paradigm (made up of scientific theories) contributes to the production of the paradigm by resolving ambiguities in the paradigm to make the paradigm stronger and more reliable.[7] At the same time, the community is applying the paradigm to solve real life problems and demonstrate that predictions of the theories in the paradigm agree with real life states of affairs in the world. These are at least two modes of thinking that occur, simultaneously, within a knowledge community. It appears that while scientists and engineers act as creators of their paradigms, they also act to apply their paradigms to solve real life problems. They do this as if their paradigms were "things" other than their own creations. However, since a paradigm is created by a knowledge community, if that community uses its own paradigm to defend its paradigm's validity, the defense is a circular argument. A *circular argument* is an argument where an assumption is made and then the very assumption that was made is argued as "true" using the same assumption as evidence—not good, but actually difficult to avoid in research! Similarly, in applying Berger and Luckmann's theory of social construction to a *belief community*, we see that a belief community produces a religious world view that provides meaning and purpose to the people in the community. The people in the belief community then experience the religious world view—composed of beliefs—as "something" other than their own creation.

What, then, is a possible relationship between knowledge communities and belief communities? Belief claims are governed by religions which teach religious or spiritual ideas about the world. This type of criterion, governing belief claims, functions in a similar way to the criterion governing knowledge claims in science. For, as we have seen, knowledge claims in science are governed by paradigms which teach scientific or technical ideas about the world. So, it appears that neither scientific knowledge nor religious knowledge is completely free from the influence of one particular knowledge or belief community. If we change our scientific paradigm and move to a different knowledge community (which uses a different paradigm), we end up questioning the acceptability of our original knowledge claims. If we change our religion and move to a different belief community, we end up questioning the acceptability of our original belief claims. A relationship between knowledge communities and belief communities is that both communities are structured around the same *form* of *thinking*—a form of thinking which depends on some type of previous *foundation*. We have foundations of scientific research (knowledge communities) and we have foundations of mythological narratives (belief communities). I express the relationship between knowledge and belief communities in the following dictum: Change your scientific paradigm and you re-evaluate your knowledge claims; change your religion and you re-evaluate your belief claims.

Proponents of social construction, when applied to knowledge and belief communities, are aware that social construction is open to critique. Through my application of Berger and Luckmann's theory of social construction to knowledge and belief communities, another person could argue that I, too, am "trapped" inside my own particular world view and, therefore, I have created the idea that social construction is a legitimate or useful theory. Perhaps this is a type of critique that all of us must face at one time or another in whatever work we do. Indeed, the author of any book, in one way or another, always risks the possibility of this type of criticism. Even if an author makes his or her own assumptions clear, assumptions are still assumptions, placing the author within one particular school of thought. This, however, is a good demonstration for why stating one's assumptions is important, because the stating of assumptions does make clear the foundations behind one's argument. Is this another lesson for the adjudicator? Yes, the lesson here is that assumptions matter. Don't ever let anyone tell you otherwise. But, in regards to the problem that I, too, might be "trapped" inside my own world view, I acknowledge that, yes, in writing this book I possess my own world view. I exist within the world view of a neutral, dispassionate, and unbiased observer who evaluates the merits of knowledge and belief claims as an outsider. I don't profess to be a member of any one particular knowledge or belief system, but instead I remain *neutral*. (When I was setting up our adventure at the beginning of the book, I encouraged all of us to consider becoming neutral, dispassionate, and unbiased observers.)

I can hear my critics. I am very much aware that someone might ask me the following questions: Does not your decision to be a neutral, dispassionate, and unbiased observer also make you, automatically, a member of a type of "knowledge and belief system" which is defined by *neutrality* and *dispassionate* and *"unbiased"* thinking? So, you are actually no more neutral or unbiased than anyone else who chooses to, say, be a member of a "knowledge and belief system" based on theism or atheism? Well, what I can say in response to such questions is that at least my choice to be a neutral, dispassionate, and unbiased observer allows me the option of being open to modification of my own world view. I am allowing myself an attitude of accepting that all knowledges and beliefs are corrigible, which, as mentioned before, means that all knowledges and beliefs have the potential to be corrected or tweaked. As I've said throughout our adventure, acknowledging this type of attitude of mind is the very definition of *rationality* (*rational*) itself. A large part of our adventure is to develop an attitude of mind that allows us space in our minds to make changes to our world views and, if needed, to re-evaluate the acceptability of our own knowledges and beliefs. By acting as a neutral, dispassionate, and unbiased observer, I keep myself open to many world view options. I may even end up formulating a new world view in the future, incorporating elements of various knowledge and belief identities, such as the atheist, theist, agnostic, or igtheist identities. I can learn to acknowledge that all of these identities are, at one time or another, useful. This is learning at its best, because it is a type of learning about the world that arises from real life experience.

In our everyday learning we need opportunities to work out inconsistencies and mistakes as we uncover them. This leads us, ultimately, to deeper and more mature understandings of the world. A denial of this type of attitude of mind is a denial of the purpose of learning, a denial of intellect, and a denial of ourselves. So, my final defense of the world view I chose in writing this book: I don't want to be a person who denies the purpose of learning! Instead I want to utilize the rationality that the gods (*elohim*) gave to human beings when the gods created human beings in their image, as narrated in the mythological story of the Garden of Eden (the ancient Hebrew word *elohim* in the Hebrew creation narrative translates as *gods* in English). From here I may grow into a life of faith that connects me with the mysteries of a transempirical world, and in general the possibility of a "world" beyond the visible world. Faith, expressed by a willingness to be open to the ideas of eternity as symbolized in the myth of the Tree of Life, might even be what grounds my desire to learn from experience—my acknowledgement that there are things that I cannot know about myself and others, but faith opens me up to maybe getting a bit of a grasp of those things. And, even if I end up having to say that "God" does not exist (because to believe in something I have never seen is really so hard for me to do), the action of faith that I possess in my life opens me up to the real "GOD" who is beyond my grasp of knowledge; the real "GOD" who I cannot really ever know or understand. I can never stop growing in a relationship with this "GOD"—the "GOD" who escapes the boundaries of my human mind and the boundaries of human knowledge.

To wrap up this chapter, how can we experience a common ground among knowledge communities (science) and belief communities (religion)? A science and religion compatibility system based on similarities between knowledge and belief communities has been proposed by various people. In academic books it is not an uncommon compatibility system, but I will also point out it has not been used very much in books that are available to a wide audience of readers. Nevertheless scholars including Hans Küng,[8] Ian Barbour,[9] and Donald Wiebe[10] have proposed compatibility systems based on knowledge and belief communities (Wiebe has since abandoned a compatibility system), and although I present my own take on knowledge and belief communities in this book, I have benefited from reading the works of these authors. The following is a summary of my own perspective on knowledge and belief communities: Scientific thinking is a type of thinking that people of different religions are more likely to share. Unlike religious thinking, which derives from mythological narratives and is specific to each belief community, scientific thinking is more easily shared by all. To illustrate this point, it is no problem for high school, college, or university students of different religions to come together in a chemistry laboratory to complete an experiment. It is understood that the scientific method, undertaken in a school to complete an experiment, is not influenced by one's religion. So, students of different religions are free to work together on the experiment without any compromising issues being at stake. Also, it seems that when people hear the topic of "science and religion" mentioned, they imagine something along the lines of science being used to attempt to explain the content of religious narratives. It is clear in our adventure that this is not our purpose; however, what is helpful (I trust) is our exploration into some of the philosophical aspects of scientific and religious lives. Finding connections between science and religion in ways that avoid direct examples from either science or religion, but instead apply the similarity between knowledge communities (science) and belief communities (religion) may open up doors for all of us to find meaning and purpose in our lives and, most importantly, bring people from diverse scientific and religious backgrounds closer together. The realization that knowledge communities are similar to belief communities, as described in this chapter, may help all of us to be more interested in hearing about each other's human knowledges and beliefs. Remember the following dictum mentioned earlier in this chapter: "Change your scientific paradigm and you re-evaluate your knowledge claims; change your religion and you re-evaluate your belief claims." Both knowledge and belief communities are structured around the same form of thinking which depends on a previous foundation—scientific research (knowledge communities) or mythological narratives (belief communities).

My brief homiletic statement is as follows (the only one you'll find in this book, but I was a preacher once so I am sometimes inclined toward this type of pastoral discourse): There are various ways in which we can catch glimpses of the "truths" of empirical or trans-empirical worlds whether they are through scientific or religious "lenses." An awareness of this diversity in ourselves and others can enrich our lives, helping to bring knowledge and belief communities closer together. By approaching the problem of a compatibility system between science and religion in this way, we experience life as *scientific-religious theologians*—people who are both scientific and religious at the same time. This is the postmodernist view of knowledge (not without its critics) which suggests that the barriers preventing some types of knowledge—e.g. religious knowledge—from counting as legitimate forms of knowledge have gradually fallen away or should fall away. Whether or not we live in a postmodern age (or whether we should) is open to debate. The answers you get on this will vary depending with whom you speak. For myself, I don't always know what I think about the postmodernist view of knowledge. However, with the option available to us of utilizing both scientific "lenses" and religious "lenses," let us move forward to Part III, *Adjudicators*.

NOTES

1. Thomas S. Kuhn, *The Structure of Scientific Revolutions*, 4th ed. (Chicago: The University of Chicago Press, 2012), 25–27.
2. Kuhn, *The Structure of Scientific Revolutions*, 27.
3. Ibid., 10.
4. Ibid., 24.
5. Ibid., 34.
6. Ibid., 83.
7. Ibid., 27.
8. Hans Küng, *Theology for the Third Millennium*, trans. Peter Heinegg (New York: Doubleday, 1988), 123ff.
9. Ian Barbour, *Religion and Science: Historical and Contemporary Issues* (New York: HarperCollins, 1997), 93ff.
10. Donald Wiebe, "Science and Religion: Is Compatibility Possible?" in *Beyond Legitimation: Essays on the Problem of Religious Knowledge* (New York: St. Martin's Press, Inc., 1994), 72.

III

Adjudicators

Chapter Nine

Causes and Explanatory Forces

In 1953 the novelist Aldous Huxley (who wrote the novel *Antic Hay* mentioned in Chapter Two) performed an experiment where he swallowed a small fraction of the drug mescaline dissolved in half a glass of water. The purpose of his investigation was to attempt an entry into some "inner" worlds—mystical realms—which, for Huxley, were the worlds depicted by William Blake in Blake's paintings. However, as Huxley describes in his book *The Doors of Perception* (1954): "what I had expected [admittance to an 'inner' world] did not happen."[1] The effects of the mescaline on his cognitive function were more along the lines of his viewing a slow dance of golden lights, bright nodes of swelling energy, and emerging grey structures—changes in the perception of his physical "outside" world rather than exposure to mystical "inner" worlds.[2] The mescaline experiments of Huxley and similar experiments at the time opened up a range of speculation concerning the types of worlds that we've been calling trans-empirical worlds: Do trans-empirical worlds exist? Can the ingestion of a psychotropic drug provide admittance to such a world? Do changes in cognitive function caused by chemical reactions in the human brain have something to do with a trans-empirical world? I would add, what about when someone drinks a nice glass of scotch over ice and the drink gradually works its magic—is that experience, produced by the ingestion of the scotch, a type of trans-empirical world? Or, are all of these questions really quite silly?

At any rate, whether you find the questions in the preceding paragraph silly, or not, we as human beings have always desired to seek out and understand the mysterious. From his own perspective on the relationships between science, art, and the world, the physicist Albert Einstein remarked, "The fairest thing we can experience is the mysterious. It is the fundamental emotion which stands at the cradle of true art and true science."[3] Many scientific theories have been answers to human mysteries. Many paintings and other works of art have been responses to human mysteries. And, many religious and philosophical teachings have been visible expressions of human mysteries. In fact, a trans-empirical world may be thought of as a type of *mystery* and this is perhaps the best analogy we should adopt moving forward toward the end of our adventure. What is a mystery? For Hercule Poirot, the fictional detective developed by the writer Agatha Christie, a mystery would be something that needs to be unravelled from within, a job for Poirot's "little grey cells" (his working brain). Although Poirot was always solving complicated murder mysteries, he may be on to something deeper. For, whether a crime mystery or not, how can a mystery be explained unless we get to the very heart of the mystery by looking inside of the mystery? To explain the mystery of a trans-empirical world, we need to get inside of a trans-empirical world and then unravel it from within. Scientific theories, paintings and works of art, and religious and philosophical teachings, have all been ways that people have tried to delve into the mystery of a trans-empirical or invisible world. Even science, which is innately empirical and based on the observable world, can be a search for the mysterious. We might consider the possibility that the activity of science came into existence because people wondered about the mysterious. The activity of religion certainly came into existence for the same reason.

When we talk about mysteries we end up, inevitably, talking about truths. Behind every mystery lies a truth. Throughout our adventure we've been giving considerable attention to what exactly it means to know the truth—what does it mean to know reality as reality is? If we could know reality as reality is, we'd also probably know the truth. It doesn't seem right to say that truth is merely a description of reality or a model for reality. Truth needs to be *knowledge* of reality—knowledge of reality *as* reality is. The problem is, given our limitations as human beings and the fact that all knowledge will always have the potential to be corrected (all knowledge is corrigible), we may never actually get to the point of really possessing knowledge of reality as reality is. Thus, we may never get to the point of really knowing the one and only "truth," if there indeed is such a thing. (Sometimes in this book I put the word *truth* in quotation marks. I sometimes put the word *truth* in quotation marks to point out the vagueness of truth—to make the point that the idea of truth may be a meaningless idea.) In searching for truth, we may have to settle for something else—perhaps a description of reality or a model for reality, even if those things may seem unconvincing. One way to go is to apply the so-called *correspondence* view of truth, where truth is a description of reality which consistently describes reality independent of how we ourselves think about reality. In the correspondence view of truth, our thoughts about reality could be totally off, but so long as we have figured out accurate descriptions of reality (independent of our thoughts), then we are okay. It is possible that we figured out accurate descriptions of reality by testing knowledge claims in a scientific experiment—keeping some knowledge claims and throwing the rest away. Another way to go is to apply the so-called *pragmatic* view of truth, where truth is assessed, not by how well it describes reality, but by how well it accomplishes a task or provides a useful model for us. If you think back to Chapter Two, when we discussed various ways to understand scientific theories, you will notice how the correspondence view of truth is very similar to the way a classical realist understands scientific theories. For a classical realist, scientific theories are physical descriptions of reality as reality is. Also, the pragmatic view of truth is very similar to the way an instrumentalist understands scientific theories. For an instrumentalist, scientific theories serve as useful models for predicting states of affairs in the world.

Earlier on, we considered the possibility that there is not one type of truth in the world, but many types of truths just as there are many types of knowledges and beliefs. (Do you remember philosopher of science Thomas Kuhn's philosophy of paradigms, where the paradigm that you are working under determines what the "truth" is?) There are also many different human mysteries about the world, so from that perspective it makes sense that there could be many different truths. It is not my purpose in this book to offer a strategy for figuring out the most "correct" truth about the world, if there is such a thing. If that were my purpose I don't think I would even know where to begin, because, with truth, we are dealing with a problem that might be, in itself, meaningless. For some people, the notion of a most "correct" truth is meaningless. They feel the question "what is the most 'correct' truth?" is a meaningless question, because how can we discuss the most "correct" truth before we have reached a consensus on what exactly we mean by the word *truth*? Nevertheless there are also a lot of people out there who search for and have a belief about the existence of a most "correct" truth—an absolute truth. If you happen to be one of those people, then I do wish you well in your searching. My only advice on this matter is that we shouldn't ever let anyone else tell us *what* or *where* truth is. Scientists who have put their whole "faith" in science and science alone, religious fanatics who believe that only their religious perspective is right and other religions are wrong, and anyone who rigidly adheres to any kind of dogma—any of these people might be folks who are trying to market their own absolute truth as the *only* truth. Be wary of such individuals! Most of us pity them.

In the late 19th century and early 20th century, a field of academic study called the scientific study of religion was developed. In various forms, this field continues in the 21st century. Scholars who teach and work in this field have decided (for the most part) that the dogmatic premise of religious *truth* is best not assumed or used as an explanatory force in academic work. *Explanatory force* is a fancy phrase which could also be called *explanation*.

However I use the phrase *explanatory force*, because it carries greater weight than *explanation*. There are two reasons for this, which are as follows:

1. The term *explanation* is usually reserved for the scientific or engineering disciplines where it is understood that we are looking for mechanistic answers (explanations) for causes of states of affairs in the world. As mentioned before, in those cases, we are asking "how" questions (and only "how" questions).
2. If we are not looking to answer "how" questions only, but are also looking to provide answers based on invisible causes, then we are in fact "forcing" ourselves to utilize an explanation about the gods, an answer to a "who" question. Furthermore an explanation about the gods carries a great weight or *force*—it is difficult to be critical of an explanation involving the gods, because the gods are invisible and we cannot say one way or the other if they exist.

So, if we choose to use religious *truth* as an explanation in our academic work, as a cause for why certain events occur in the world, we have to "force" ourselves to invoke the gods. As mentioned, we cannot test whether or not the gods exist. For this reason we had better ask ourselves whether or not we should really be using the gods (religious *truth*) as an explanatory force? Like all decisions in this adventure, I'll leave that decision up to you. At least now you understand the implications of using religious truth, or not, in your own work.

As you might have guessed, the scientific study of religion uses a variety of academic subjects—philosophy, psychology, anthropology, and cognitive science—to provide scientific explanations for religious activity. The scientific study of religion doesn't say one way or the other whether a god or gods exist. That, in itself, would be irresponsible scientific work, because any "theory" about a god or gods does not have the potential to be found to be false. If you recall from earlier discussion, for a scientific theory to be tested (and therefore useful) the theory must have the potential to be found to be false. There are a lot of "theories" out there in the world, which do not have the potential to be found to be false. That is okay. Those theories are not scientific theories, but they are "theories." Science is concerned only with scientific theories, which have the potential to be found to be false. Other domains of knowledge, such as the domain of religious knowledge, are concerned with other "theories" (which do not have the potential to be found to be false).

Why doesn't a "theory" about a god or gods have the *potential* to be found to be false? For a theory to have the potential to be found to be false, we need to have some physical phenomenon that our theory cannot explain or solve. We need to know what that phenomenon is ahead of time. When we talk about a god or gods, in a trans-empirical world, is there any physical phenomenon that a god or gods cannot explain or solve? Maybe there is or maybe there is not. The problem is, we have no idea! So, a theory about a god or gods doesn't have the potential to be found to be false. Also, I must emphasize that the scientific study of religion doesn't seek to belittle or mock religion. After all, these are scholars who have chosen to invest their teaching and research careers on a topic that is, fundamentally, about religion and religiosity. If those people really didn't think religion or religiosity might have a purpose on earth, they probably would have chosen to focus their careers somewhere else. What these scholars don't like, however, is when rationality is thrown out the door; when religious teachings (some of which can be quite sexist, racist, and homophobic) are taught as if they are the absolute truth. (In actuality, there are no scientific reasons for adhering so strictly to any religious dogma, without any room for at least some debate.) As Wiebe points out, science has been the only institution to consciously allow "learning from experience" to be its primary goal.[4] We've said it before and let's say it again: without an attitude of mind that allows for modification of one's own beliefs and world views, which is accomplished through the testing of knowledge, learning cannot be accomplished. To that point, I also have to ask: why would religious people not also desire to embrace this model for learning? This is just something to think about. If you agree with me, that's great. If you don't agree with me, I am sorry. But, hey, even religious sermons are meant to make the people in the pews uncomfortable! If you really, really don't agree with me, then perhaps you might take what I've said here, use it to really understand the premises of the scientific study of religion, and then write your own book which counteracts what I have said here. Really, I mean it.

Cognitive scientist Pascal Boyer, in his book *Religion Explained: The Evolutionary Origins of Religious Thought* (2001), offers his own thoughts about using cognitive science to "explain" religion. Using epistemology, we must consider what aspects of an "explanation" are needed to adequately justify an explanation as a scientific explanation. An explanation—or, in Latin, the *explanans*—serves as the justification for a knowledge claim. In Western research, an explanation is usually empirical. An explanation that is empirical is based on the observed world. As I see it, an explanation must accomplish the following goals:

1. An explanation reveals the *cause* for how something happened.
2. An explanation articulates the *cause* in a meaningful or useful way for human beings.
3. If possible, an explanation presents a *cause* which can be repeated and reproduced artificially during an experiment. This ensures that the cause is a justified cause.

The search for causes, which is called the causal theory of knowledge, depends upon empirical evidence. There must be something visible in the natural world that is observed or tested using scientific methods (rather than deferring to only religious perceptions, an unwarranted assumption, or mere guesswork). As you've probably realized, many explanations provided in some academic subjects are not necessarily based on empirical evidence. However, what I am stressing here is that empirical explanations are the benchmark of the science and engineering subjects.

Traditionally, most psychological "explanations" for religion were based on generalizations (though useful ones), such that religion is well suited to the lives of human beings: human minds readily desire explanations, human societies prefer order, and human beings seek comfort.[5] (That human beings seek *comfort* is similar to philosopher Bertrand Russell's more skeptically phrased explanation for religion where religion provides the notion of a "big brother who will look after you."[6]) Pascal Boyer is cautious of these traditional psychological explanations for religion, because he feels they do not account for why religion exists in the particular *ways* that it exists. Also these psychological explanations seem to be reflections about religion made by religious people only after those people decided to live a religious life. The core of Boyer's work is that he offers a different *cause* for religion—a cause derived from cognitive science. Similar to the notion that all human beings have the capability of catching a seasonal cold (because we already possess the necessary vulnerabilities of a respiratory system), we are presented by Boyer with the idea that all human beings possess a cognitive capacity to acquire religion.[7] This conclusion is supported by the fact that our minds are prepared in a specific way, through evolution, to be most suited toward specific mental concepts. Special variations of these mental concepts seem to coalesce well with the nature of religious thought.

Using the understanding from cognitive science of various "explanatory engines" in the human mind, we learn from Boyer that religious notions, which appear ordinary, may derive from one kind of "explanatory engine." (Other "explanatory engines" include mental systems responsible for psychological, biological, or mechanical information.) Much of this activity, deriving from various "explanatory engines," occurs in our unconscious "mental basement," separated from conscious thought. Despite the principles of reason and rationality, it seems a lot of random information enters our minds, providing fodder for our minds and impacting its contents in some way. In many religious traditions, beliefs about gods are beliefs about superhuman agents who are thought to be similar to human beings, but possess properties distinguishing them from human beings. In other cases there are people who possess beliefs about ghosts—the kinds of ghosts that are dead people who make appearances to living people, as is the case with Jacob Marley's ghost in Charles Dickens' *A Christmas Carol*. From Boyer, we learn how, when the category of "human being" is mixed with an unusual property (perhaps the ability to appear and disappear at whim), the outcome produced, is, say, the category of "ghost." Our human minds then apply to ghosts attributes which human beings possess. So, sure, ghosts are not meant to be the same as human beings, but our minds seem to naturally assume that ghosts must, for example, be able to remember previous events. Even if people have not been told that so-called ghosts can remember previous events, our minds may default to this assumption, because human beings can remember previous events and ghosts are produced through a mixing of the category of "human being" with an unusual property. That is enough rambling about ghosts, however, the point to be made here is that our human minds seem to latch on to this kind of thinking: We seem very inclined to experience beliefs about supernatural phenomena, especially when those phenomena include a mixing of our own category "human being" with an unusual property. These are some of the conclusions reached when providing an explanation for religion through cognitive science.

The idea of speculative thought is another way to help us distinguish scientific knowledge from other *types* of knowledges. Speculative thought helps us to understand the nature of causes and explanatory forces and how these function differently in the realms of science and religion. When we speculate on something, we usually end up formulating a hypothesis about the topic in question. Like all thinking, speculation provides a way for us to move beyond observed experience and then provide structure and analysis to our experience. Only then can we begin to test our knowledge, with the option of, ultimately, accepting or discarding our initial hypothesis. Speculative thought is comprised of a variety of features, including the formation of hypotheses, structure, order, and logical coherence—features which characterize a transition from chaos into order. However, what if we choose not to test our hypothesis? What if we choose to speculate, moving beyond our experience, but then we stop there? Our choice to either test our hypothesis, or not, is what determines the type of knowledge we eventually will possess. It is difficult to imagine speculating about ourselves (I mean really speculating about our own existence), but this may be one example where religion comes into play. Religious knowledge, developed in its various forms and from various historical traditions, plays the role of doing the speculating for us. It seems this process of speculating about oneself was quite straightforward in the ancient world. For the most part, in ancient civilizations, the realm of the natural world and the realm of human beings were indistinguishable. From our perspective, the only drawback for such a scenario would be that scientific methods, which allow for testing knowledge, are not so clear when the natural world and human beings are indistinguishable. If human beings are indistinguishable from the natural world, then how can human beings speculate about the natural world? How can human beings even test their hypotheses about the natural world? In a previous section, I said, "For the ancient mind, the natural world, external to you or me, is 'alive' and changing—not changing because of mechanical forces, chemical reactions, or evolutionary biology, but changing because the natural world is full of gods. These gods cause events to occur in the world. In contrast, as a modern human being with a modern mind, I do not see the external world as being 'alive,' but rather I understand causes of events using scientific theories. These causes might involve mechanical forces, chemical reactions, or evolutionary biology. In a later chapter, called *Causes and Explanatory Forces*, we will revisit some of these ideas." Well, my friends, now indeed is the time to revisit these ideas about causes and explanatory forces.

It seems the main distinction between causes and explanatory forces for the ancient mind and causes and explanatory forces for the modern mind is that the ancient mind cannot get itself "out" of the natural phenomenon under study. It's not that ancient humans were necessarily unable to be rational (possessing an attitude of mind that keeps us open to change), but in their world view where the natural world was not distinguished from themselves they could not allow themselves to be separated from the phenomenon under study. To separate themselves from any natural phenomenon would be just too impersonal. (For them, it was probably out of the question.) In such a world view, what is left to be a cause or explanatory force? We've pretty well exhausted the form of causes and explanatory forces in modern science, but what about ancient mythological thinking? We did mention the use of "who" and "why" questions and how these questions still permeate religious thinking today. The questions "who caused an event to occur?" or "why did an event occur?" are typical questions for the ancient mind and for modern religion, both of which are conditioned by mythological thinking. Another element that distinguishes causes for the ancient mind is the element of emotion. In a world where every event is so personal, the contribution of emotion prevents any kind of neutrality. To put it another way, among early prehistoric people we probably wouldn't have found many (if any) neutral, dispassionate, and unbiased adjudicators of human knowledges and beliefs. Perhaps they were their own adjudicators in some way, but the idea of removing themselves from knowledges and beliefs, and then placing knowledge or belief claims under scrutiny, was probably foreign to them. Moreover, if presented with the idea, they probably wouldn't have liked it. (I don't know what they would say about this book or our adventure, especially when we are trying to measure the acceptability of knowledges and beliefs in a neutral fashion.)

Before the end we will look more closely at some other forms of ancient knowledge, taking us back to about 2,500 years ago when rational, pre-scientific thinking begins to appear in classical antiquity. For now, the important points to remember are that causes and explanatory forces in the ancient mind are personal and emotional: they are about asking "who" and "why" questions. The modern mind may be able to ask "who" and "why" questions, but the modern mind can also ask "how" questions. Asking "how" questions is possible, because of modern science. Our exploration in this chapter, into some "explanations" for religion from psychological and cognitive sciences, has helped us to see that we can ask "how" questions about religion. What this means, however, is that we have to take a step back and look at religion from the "outside," working as neutral, dispassionate, and unbiased observers. Most importantly, we also need some standards to measure the acceptability or legitimacy of our human knowledges and beliefs. Learning about and developing those standards, by using epistemology (the *form of knowledge*), is what the preceding chapters of this book were all about. Now has come the time to put what we have learned to use. So, go and grab a glass of water or wine, a cup of coffee or tea, or whatever you prefer. I'll meet you back here as soon as you are ready for the next chapter!

NOTES

1. Aldous Huxley, *The Doors of Perception* (New York: HarperCollins, 1954), 15.
2. Huxley, *The Doors of Perception*, 16.
3. Albert Einstein, *The World As I See It* (1949; repr., New York: Kensington Publishing Corp., 1984), 7.
4. Donald Wiebe, *The Irony of Theology and the Nature of Religious Thought* (Montreal: McGill-Queen's University Press, 1991), 38.
5. Pascal Boyer, *Religion Explained: The Evolutionary Origins of Religious Thought* (New York: Basic Books, 2001), 5.
6. Bertrand Russell, *Why I Am Not a Christian* (New York: Simon and Schuster, 1957), 14.
7. Boyer, *Religion Explained*, 4.

Chapter Ten

The "Knowledge Bar"

At the end of the previous chapter we began to outline some interesting points: we began to analyze what I call the "knowledge bar," a measuring bar for knowledge claims. If your mind has been drifting for a bit (which is okay—this can happen to all of us when reading a book), this would be a good time for you to bring your attention back to our adventure—this chapter is a very important chapter. As adjudicators, we each create our own "knowledge bar." You will have your own "knowledge bar," I will have my own "knowledge bar," and everyone else reading this book will have their own "knowledge bars." Throughout the remainder of our adventure, we will begin a process to create and use our "knowledge bars." When our adventure is complete (don't worry—we still have new things to learn), this process to create and use our "knowledge bars" becomes a lifelong journey. Life always presents new opportunities to learn more about human knowledges and beliefs while also putting our "knowledge bars" to work. The role of an adjudicator is always evolving and never ends.

So, you are probably asking: what exactly is a "knowledge bar"? Put simply a "knowledge bar" is used to "measure" or adjudicate a knowledge claim—whether that be a knowledge claim in science or a knowledge claim in religion. The "knowledge bar" is not a physical measuring bar (we call it a "bar" to give it a fancy name), but a "knowledge bar" is a *series of standards* by which a knowledge claim is measured. There are two options: we measure (adjudicate) a knowledge claim to be legitimate (right, correct, and valid) or not legitimate (not right, not correct, and not valid). There may also be cases where we cannot say, one way or the other, if a knowledge claim is legitimate or not. We have the tools available to us to decide which particular standards we would each like to include in our own personal "knowledge bar." Any of the content in the preceding chapters of this book is potential content for the standards of a "knowledge bar." For example, the philosophies of science of Thomas Kuhn and Karl Popper, the theory of social construction of Peter Berger and Thomas Luckmann applied to knowledge and belief communities, or the possibility of living as *scientific-religious theologians* within a world view of knowledges and beliefs—these are all possible standards to utilize in a "knowledge bar." Choose all, choose any, or choose none. It is up to you. (You purchased the book, so I hope you pick at least one of these standards and get your money's worth!) If you like, throw in your own personal standards as well. In fact, I very much encourage you to do that. As I've said, we are each our own adjudicator, so we each need our own "knowledge bar." Having your own "knowledge bar" is very important. Next we will find out why. . . .

Harvard University researcher David Weinberger wrote an interesting book called *Too Big to Know: Rethinking Knowledge Now That the Facts Aren't the Facts, Experts Are Everywhere, and the Smartest Person in the Room Is the Room* (2011). In his book Weinberger explains how knowledge exists within the context of a *community*. For example, even Charles Darwin's book *On the Origin of Species* (1859), which outlines the theory of evolution by natural selection, was structured around the criticisms of others, placing Darwin's book and his theory of evolution (although a very good theory) in a particular social context.[1] Much of David Weinberger's work has been to evaluate the use of knowledge in social contexts. For example, he points out that prior to the existence of the internet, knowledge was passed from experts to everyone else through books and some television and radio.[2] There were not many opportunities for us to ask the experts questions or to challenge the experts. Rather the knowledge received from experts was taken for granted to be "correct." Today, through the internet, we can easily double check a knowledge claim made by an expert, author, or speaker. For example, if we read something in a book, a quick Google search can tell us if what we read is correct, or not (hence my careful editing of this book to make sure I got every date, detail, and definition correct—I know that you all can easily check anything I have said here). Also, the concept of an *expert* may be gradually becoming less important, referred to humorously in the subtitle of Weinberger's book: *Rethinking Knowledge Now That the Facts Aren't the Facts, Experts Are Everywhere, and the Smartest Person in the Room Is the Room*. As we have observed in our adventure the "knowledge bar" is set high for adjudicating which knowledge claims are justified and which are not. The "knowledge bar" needs to be set high. Functioning as our own "experts," we have given considerable attention to how important it is to separate justified beliefs from non-justified beliefs. As human beings, we believe a lot of things, but only some of those things can be counted as knowledge, at least in the strictest sense of knowledge—that is, justified belief. If you also prefer to include non-justified beliefs as a different type of knowledge, then we can utilize our comparison of *scientific knowledge* (justified belief) and *religious knowledge* (non-justified belief). However, I think we are going to find that, in most cases, the term *knowledge* is being used more and more to refer only to justified beliefs, which are the beliefs that fit into the framework of a scientific epistemology. (This is certainly the benchmark that universities and places of modern research have chosen to use.)

If each of us did not possess our own "knowledge bar," we wouldn't know how to decide consistently what counts as legitimate knowledge. The need for us to separate legitimate knowledge from knowledge that isn't legitimate is greater now in the 21st century more than ever before. Or is it? Have we actually always had this need, but perhaps just never quite realized it as being so important? Near the beginning of our adventure, in Chapter Two of Part I, I said: ". . . our roles as adjudicators come with a great responsibility—we are the people who have the task of deciding what will count as legitimate (right) knowledge and what will *not* count as legitimate knowledge. It is not just a great responsibility—it is a great *moral* responsibility. More on this later." Well, my friends, the "later" has now come. Yes, knowledge does indeed have a *moral* character. I'm not talking here about regular morals per se (e.g. it is morally wrong to kill someone). I'm talking about the fact that it is morally wrong to state that a knowledge claim is legitimate when actually it wasn't or that a knowledge claim is not legitimate when actually it was! The morality of knowledge means that knowledge itself possesses a *moral* character, as described in the sentence before. Why is it immoral to claim that knowledge is legitimate when actually it wasn't or vice versa? Well, where would we be if we didn't know what legitimate knowledge is? Being able to discern legitimate knowledge from illegitimate knowledge has allowed us to provide such things as vaccines, provide clean water to countries that need clean water, and develop strategies to help children learn mathematics and improve their reading skills where needed. These are just a few (but important) examples. I mention them, because I think these examples themselves can demonstrate why it is important to distinguish legitimate knowledge from illegitimate knowledge and how this really is a humanitarian endeavor. Does scientific knowledge have a form of knowledge that can allow us to say, with certainty, that a claim of knowledge is most likely legitimate? Yes, it does. It is the *form of knowledge* (epistemology) that allows us to learn from observed and tested experience, as we have seen in our adventure. Does religious knowledge have a *form of knowledge* that allows us to say, with certainty, that a claim of religious knowledge is most likely legitimate? No, not exactly (at least not in the same way that a scientific form of knowledge does), but religious knowledge does have its place. I will have to leave it there. I don't want to pretend that I can elaborate any further on how exactly religious knowledge works. It's not that I am anti-religious. I don't like organized religions, but I am not anti-religious and

Chapter 10

when I was growing up I was interested in wondering about religion. But, in regards to the inner workings of "religious knowledge," I'll have to leave the rest up to God. Oh my, I am now using *God* as a type of explanatory force in the exact way that I said previously in my book that I should not. Well, let this be a lesson to us all! I mean that, with all humility. Actually, are we talking here about the "God" who we think exists or are we talking about the real "GOD" who escapes the boundaries of human knowledge?

Now, the time has come for each of us to ask: what *kind* of adjudicator am I? This is the moment we have all been waiting for: At the beginning of the book I said that during our adventure we would become our own adjudicators. Throughout the preceding chapters, I presented you with various options for how one might deal with the task of adjudicating human knowledges and beliefs. There have been some questions along the way with various choices, and you were provided with opportunities to decide for yourself how you might answer if you were asked those questions. The following is a summary of questions and possible answers. More than one answer to a single question is acceptable.

1. In regards to scientific thinking, are you a classical realist, critical realist, or instrumentalist? Here is a recap of the scientific identities:

   - *Classical Realist*: You think that scientific theories provide *physical* descriptions of reality as reality is. This is the closest view to saying that scientific theories are truths.
   - *Critical Realist*: You think that scientific theories provide *abstract* descriptions of physical reality, but we might not be able to fully see reality as reality is.
   - *Instrumentalist*: You think that scientific theories serve as useful *models* for predicting states of affairs in the world; however, theories do not describe reality as reality is.

2. In regards to religious thinking, are you an atheist, theist, agnostic, or igtheist? Here is a recap of the religious identities:

   - *Atheist*: You say that you do not believe in God. Who knows what you really think? Do you even know?
   - *Theist*: You say that you believe in God. Who knows what you really think? Do you even know?
   - *Agnostic*: You say there is no way to know whether or not God exists. Who knows what you really believe? Do you even know?
   - *Igtheist*: You say that the statement *God exists* is a meaningless statement. Who knows what the word *God* really means to you? Do you even know?

3. In regards to the "knowledge bar," what standards do you include in your "knowledge bar" to adjudicate a knowledge claim in science or in religion? The following are some possible standards for your "knowledge bar." The answers (up to you) are unlimited.

- *Scientific Practice*: Do you like the philosophies of science of Thomas Kuhn and Karl Popper as developed in the 20th century and used as explanations of contemporary scientific practice?
- *Religious Life*: Do you think that religious life depends on the expression of one's faith within an institutionalized religious structure, or not? Can the expressions of faiths vary based on differences in beliefs about superhuman agents?
- *Theory of Social Construction*: Do you support the theory of social construction of Peter Berger and Thomas Luckmann applied to knowledge communities (science) and belief communities (religion)?
- *Scientific-Religious Theologians*: Do you appreciate the idea of living in the world as a *scientific-religious* theologian? Would you incorporate both knowledges and beliefs into a single world view system?

The type of adjudicator that you are will depend on which answers you prefer to the preceding questions. The number of different types of adjudicators is unlimited. Any combination of answers to the preceding questions (including combinations where you have two or more answers to a single question) will result in yet again another type of adjudicator. As we discussed, different adjudicators are distinguishable by the different types of "knowledge bars" they utilize when they adjudicate knowledges and beliefs. So, really, when we discuss different types of adjudicators we are actually discussing different types of "knowledge bars"—each with their own adjudicating standards.

The following are the profiles of some imaginary adjudicators—what they might think and how they might utilize their "knowledge bars." Keep in mind these profiles are examples only. As I said before each of us is our own adjudicator and each of us has our own "knowledge bar." This book itself serves as a starting point. You might now be inclined to continue your own research into human knowledges and beliefs or to include your own personal adjudicating standards in your own "knowledge bar." Or, you might want to remove some of the adjudicating standards I have suggested. Perhaps you are satisfied with human knowledges but don't like human beliefs or you are satisfied with human beliefs but don't like human knowledges. There are unlimited possibilities as you progress. Hopefully the following examples will help to get you started on thinking along these lines. Remember, you are your own adjudicator with your own "knowledge bar." None of us are the same adjudicator.

- *The "Cautious Believer"*: In regards to scientific thinking, you decide that most of the time you are a critical realist but other times you are an instrumentalist. These are the "lenses" through which you understand scientific theories. You will use these perspectives when you adjudicate a knowledge claim in science. In regards to religious thinking, you decide that the theory of social construction of Peter Berger and Thomas Luckmann is certainly intriguing, but you are somewhat suspicious of it. It is a theory after all and, as a good adjudicator, you know that a theory is not always the same as knowledge. You decide that you will look into this theory a bit more before you make up your mind as to whether or not to include it as an adjudicating standard in your "knowledge bar." Also, you are a conservatively religious person who feels that religious narratives are historical rather than mythological. The suggestion that you might have unknowingly created your own religious beliefs through your participation in the life of a belief community is just a bit too much to swallow. At any rate, you don't want to get onto the wrong side of God. People really shouldn't be questioning the religious beliefs they were taught as children. Still, you might just read up on that theory of social construction once more. It might have some useful points to consider.
- *The "Loyal Atheist"*: When asked about your religious identity, you say that you are an atheist. No question. Always have been and always will be. Even in your mother's womb you had this figured out! The other religious identities (theist, agnostic, or igtheist) are just silly. You are also a big fan of the philosophies of science of Thomas Kuhn and Karl Popper. Kuhn's notion of scientific paradigms and Popper's condition that a scientific theory must have the potential to be found to be false play large roles in how you function as an adjudicator. For example, you apply Popper's condition that a scientific theory must have the potential to be found to be false when you separate justified beliefs from non-justified beliefs. You have a straightforward "knowledge bar"—for you, a justified belief is a belief that arises from a scientific theory that had the potential to be found to be false. Any belief that didn't arise from a scientific theory that had the potential to be found to be false amounts to nothing more than wishful thinking. You strongly feel that the world needs more justified beliefs (knowledge) and less non-justified beliefs. We'd all be a lot smarter (and happier) if we would just accept that and move on with our lives. Still, you can't help but feel very confused when you attend funerals. Sure, everyone probably feels the same, but you can't stop wondering about where the dead person has gone? A long time ago you made yourself accept that nothing happens after death (you still think that and you are fine with

that), but somehow going to the funeral service provides you with some meaning in your own life. In that way, religion may have a purpose after all.
- *The "Free Thinker"*: An array of knowledges and beliefs in one's life is all well and good, but, really, the theory of social construction is where it's at. Peter Berger and Thomas Luckmann are your heroes. You are adamant that not one person can ever say for sure that his or her own religious beliefs are the most "correct," because how can that person know that he or she is not living a religious life that is a created product of a socially constructed reality? As an adjudicator, you decide that everyone's personal beliefs might as well be called the most "correct" beliefs, since everyone has created the beliefs they experience and we can't say one way or another who is most right. You are not opposed to the idea of "God," but your "God" is different from the traditional understanding of God. For you, "God" exists in the imagination of human minds. You don't think this is a problem (though you acknowledge it certainly is heresy from the perspective of a mainstream religious person). Rather you find the idea of "God" existing in the human imagination quite liberating! Perhaps this is what those religious prophets thought all along. If anyone accuses you of heresy, you respond by saying: how can life progress in the 21st century if we are not willing to re-evaluate our own beliefs? Anyway, this is learning from experience, which is learning at its best. You are pleased with your life as a free thinker and your "knowledge bar" allows for the acceptance of many different knowledges and beliefs.

Those are my examples. Take what you like from them. Use them as starting points, or don't use them at all. It is up to you. Also, although these examples are completely made up and do not represent the lives of real people, it is likely the case that there are real people in the world who would fit these examples quite easily. They all live in different countries, they have different jobs, and they experience different kinds of knowledges and beliefs. They are our friends, relatives, lovers, and colleagues. Life is very "grey" and rarely, if ever, simple and straightforward. So, in figuring out what kind of adjudicator you are, don't be afraid to be creative and take a risk. Life really is too short for not doing either of those. At this point, I'd suggest taking a break from reading or, if you are motivated, read through the final two chapters toward the Epilogue at the end. We are nearly there. I do hope that all of you are able to begin forming in your minds what kinds of adjudicators you are. I also hope this adventure has sparked an interest for you to look deeper into all of the possibilities for how you might adjudicate or measure human knowledges and beliefs. As mentioned, this is a lifelong journey and the process is never fully complete. In that way, it is sort of like a life of faith. Lastly I should also mention that although science is an activity which is based on tested theories (which are most likely accurate descriptions of physical reality or models for reality) that does not mean that the work of an adjudicator does not include the measuring of knowledge claims in science. As mentioned previously, with might consider that the activity of science came into existence because people wondered about the mysterious. People then wanted to provide natural explanations for states of affairs in the world—explanations which they could test using experiments. However, the mysterious is connected to science just as much as it is connected to religion. The role of an adjudicator is to work with the mysterious—analyzing the mysterious, adding to it, and shaping it. This amounts to the task of working with life and with all of life—the scientific life, the religious life, and everything else beyond.

NOTES

1. David Weinberger, *Too Big to Know: Rethinking Knowledge Now That the Facts Aren't the Facts, Experts Are Everywhere, and the Smartest Person in the Room Is the Room* (New York: Basic Books, 2011), 176.
2. Weinberger, *Too Big to Know*, 51.

Chapter Eleven

Ancient Forms of Knowledge

During this adventure, we have focused on contemporary forms of knowledge. This has been a reasonable thing to do, since we ourselves live in the present age and our ability to function as good adjudicators depends on our ability to understand contemporary forms of knowledge. The human race has spent a lot of time coming up with the forms of knowledge we have been learning. It would be a shame if we weren't aware of the progress that has been made over the years in the area of epistemology (the *form of knowledge*). Luckily for us, we are now very much aware of this progress. Throughout this book, we have all received a good summary of contemporary epistemology as it relates to science and religion and to knowledge and belief communities. In this chapter we will discuss ancient forms of knowledge. The term *ancient* in this context deserves an explanation. In previous sections, we discussed the "ancient" human mind, which took us back to a time about 100,000 years ago. That was one use of the term *ancient*. In this chapter, the term *ancient* has a different meaning. In this chapter, "*ancient* forms of knowledge" refers to the knowledges of classical antiquity, which for us begins about 2,500 years ago and occurs exclusively in what is now present-day Europe.

In the previous chapter, I remarked: "The need for us to separate legitimate knowledge from knowledge that isn't legitimate is greater now in the 21st century more than ever before. Or is it?" I then went on to discuss the moral character of knowledge; however, at that point I didn't really discuss whether or not the need to separate legitimate knowledge from knowledge that isn't legitimate is a new need or a need that might have existed before, even in ancient times. Let us jump back, 2,500 years or so, and take a look at what was happening at that time in Miletus—an ancient intellectual hub, the location of which is found in present-day Turkey. In his research, our 20th century philosopher of science, Karl Popper, suggested that some ancient philosophers, including a philosopher Thales, who lived in Miletus in the sixth century B.C.E., functioned in similar ways to contemporary philosophers of science. Popper suggested that these ancient philosophers (called Presocratic philosophers because they lived and died before the philosopher Socrates lived or they lived during Socrates' time but were not influenced by Socrates) offered a scientific approach to obtain knowledge of states of affairs in the world. Their approach was a tradition of critical discussion[1]—a view that the criticism of knowledges and beliefs should be tolerated. This is similar to our contemporary view of science where we learn from observed and tested experience. A spirit of critical discussion is what allows a group of people (ancient or contemporary) to learn from each other. A healthy (useful) critical discussion is the medium through which knowledges and beliefs are corrected or tweaked. I can make a knowledge or belief claim and, if you want to criticize it, you can. I listen to your criticism and then, if I choose to, I can criticize your criticism, and so on. The idea here is that throughout this process of mutual criticism, any inconsistencies or mistakes in my original knowledge or belief claim are uncovered and fixed. This is a good process for separating legitimate knowledge from knowledge that isn't legitimate.

If Popper was right and a critical approach to knowledge was being developed in Miletus in the sixth century B.C.E., then perhaps in this part of the ancient world, at this particular time, there was some form of ancient distinction between scientific (critical) knowledge and religious (non-critical) knowledge. Unlike scientific knowledge, religious knowledge is non-critical—it always seems difficult to convince another religious person, through *critical* discussion, that his or her own religious knowledge (beliefs) might need some tweaking. Likewise we don't allow other people to convince us, through critical discussion, that our own religious knowledge (beliefs) might need some tweaking. The suggestion that Miletus in the sixth century B.C.E. was similar to our own scientific age is a very intriguing thought. It means that we are not the only generation of human beings (throughout the last century and now) who have possessed the need to separate legitimate knowledge from knowledge that isn't legitimate. Thales and his ancient philosopher friends likely beat us to that and who knows who else before them? I wonder what our primitive human ancestors, the Neanderthals, thought about knowledge? It has been suggested the Neanderthals had a system of language. If they had a language, perhaps they also had some type of framework for knowledge? We'll probably never know for sure.

Thales died around the year 545 B.C.E. Let's move ahead just over 100 years from then, and we reach the lifetime of the ancient Greek philosopher Plato (b. circa 429 B.C.E., d. circa 347 B.C.E.), who was mentored by Socrates. The philosopher Grace Jantzen, mentioned earlier in this book and known for her work on religious mysticism, reminds us that we cannot read

Plato's writings in a modern, Western setting without our own conditioned world views affecting our understanding.[2] Plato's view of knowledge is very different from our contemporary view of knowledge. In Plato's view of knowledge a person must possess *desire* to receive knowledge by being united with the knowledge of Plato's Forms[3] (an explanation coming up soon). It is contemplation of Plato's Forms—an ancient philosophical exercise of reflective thinking—that is the strategy through which a person is united with an object of knowledge. Contemporary knowledge, on the other hand, exists in a different type of knowledge framework. With contemporary knowledge, a person possesses a human mind which actively grasps the object of knowledge to be known and then utilizes the new knowledge to accomplish some task.

Here is an explanation of Plato's Forms: Plato's Forms ("the Forms") are like a type of "heaven" and some philosophers refer to the Forms colloquially as "Plato's Heaven." The idea of Plato's Forms is that each physical object that human beings see on earth is actually an imperfect copy of the perfect Form of each object, residing outside the visible world. So, for example, I can see my physical computer on my desk, but my computer is actually an imperfect copy of the perfect Form of "computer-ness," which resides outside the visible world (Plato of course wouldn't have used the example of a computer; perhaps for him the example was a writing tablet). Hey, doesn't all of this sound something like Plato's version of an adjudicator? If you like, this is where ancient Greek philosophy and the work of an adjudicator meet. However, it is interesting that the philosopher Plato, in developing his own ideas about knowledge, turns away from the earlier ideas of Thales which are ideas of critical discussion. Instead Plato searches for knowledge through contemplation of the Forms. (Also, not only does contemplation of the Forms provide a new view of knowledge for the ancient Greek, it also ensures some form of religious afterlife.) For Plato's view of knowledge, the greatest difference from Thales' view of knowledge is perhaps that in Plato's view of knowledge there is no element of critical discussion, at least not in the sense that critical discussion is present in Thales' view of knowledge. Thales formulates a scientific hypothesis, presents it to others, and then *expects* others to criticize it (all in the spirit of learning from tested experience). Plato isn't exactly doing that when he contemplates the Forms. He is performing his own kind of reflective thinking instead. The preceding examples of Thales' and Plato's respective views of knowledge allow us to see that the ancients had a variety of options available to them for deciding what counted as knowledge and what did not count. Within only about a hundred years' time between the lives of Thales and Plato, we see significant and sudden changes in the ways that knowledge was sought out and obtained in the ancient world. The reasons for those sudden changes remain a mystery.

The theologian Augustine of Hippo (b. 354, d. 430), who lived in North Africa in the fourth and fifth centuries C.E., spent much time wondering about how knowledge of "God" might be possible? Augustine was an ancient adjudicator, though whether or not he thought of himself as an adjudicator we don't know. In his writings called the *Soliloquies*, Augustine describes a struggle between three characters who are named Augustine (himself), "Reason," and "God." The theme of this struggle, which is captured through an imaginary dialogue between Augustine and "Reason," is that of Augustine's dilemma: he would like to develop a strategy for how human beings might possess knowledge of "God," but he is having a difficult time. Like any knowledge framework (we've seen various knowledge frameworks throughout this book), Augustine's desire to know "God" means that Augustine must develop a religious language to translate his non-tested, religious experience of "God" into human words that can be spoken to another human being. In the *Soliloquies*, Augustine says to God, "Let thy door be opened to me when I knock. Teach me how to come to thee. I have nothing else but the will to come."[4] Augustine's willingness to search for guidance while covering all of the options to experience the life of God (belief, trust, and faith) appears admirable. He is honest about the nature of the imaginary conversation between himself and Reason: "They [Soliloquies] were written as a dialogue between myself and Reason, as if there were two of us present, though actually I was alone."[5] Although he is alone in his quest, we get the sense that perhaps the character "Reason" is really another part of Augustine, speaking from within, perhaps even a representation of "God" trying to bring out the answers in Augustine. At any rate, it is left somewhat unclear as to who Augustine takes the character "Reason" to represent. In the *Soliloquies*, Augustine wonders what is a satisfying knowledge of "God"? The character "Reason" responds to this dilemma by saying to Augustine: "Begin your quest, then. But first explain what manner of demonstration of God would appear to you satisfying."[6] However, Augustine seems unprepared to know what kind of demonstration of knowledge would be satisfying. Indeed there are many problems about how knowledge of "God" would be satisfying knowledge. One problem is how can "God" be an object of knowledge if we don't know what or who "God" is? Another problem is that human words are limited. "God" is unlimited, so how can human words explain what or who "God" is? As is the case for all of us, these problems are difficult to fully work out. Perhaps the maturity lies not so much in believing that coming up with solutions to these problems is possible, but acknowledging that asking these questions and wondering about these questions is how the most useful learning is accomplished.

To finish up this chapter, here is a question for us to ponder: did the ancients perform scientific experiments? Yes, probably. They wouldn't have been very much like our own experiments today, but there are some interesting examples from the ancient world of what we call thought experiments—"experiments" performed in one's imagination. There are also ancient examples of scientific hypotheses. The philosopher Thales, who was also an engineer, presented a hypothesis that the earth remains in its place, because it floats on water just as a ship floats on water.[7] Although he couldn't physically test his hypothesis, he did leave his hypothesis open to the test of *criticism*. It appears that what ended up happening was that Thales' student, Anaximander, presented a different hypothesis which was a criticism of Thales' hypothesis.[8] Anaximander decided that if the earth is supported by water, then something else would need to support the water, and so on. This was Anaximander's criticism of Thales' hypothesis. So, instead, what Anaximander proposed was that the earth is shaped like a drum at equal distance away from everything else in the universe.[9] In this way the earth has no preferred direction in which it can topple over. No, these hypotheses are nothing like contemporary scientific hypotheses and, yes, they sound a bit silly. But, these hypotheses are open to criticism, making their form similar to the form of contemporary scientific hypotheses.

An example of an ancient thought experiment might be the "Growing Argument," explained through the story of Theseus' ship as told in the ancient historian Plutarch's *Parallel Lives* (1st century C.E.). What happens in the story of Theseus' ship is that old planks of wood are removed from a ship and new planks of wood are added to replace the old planks. The question is whether or not Theseus' ship is still the same ship after the old planks have been removed and the new planks added? In this ancient thought experiment, all that is needed to perform the experiment is that we imagine the scenario of Theseus' ship in our imaginations and then we use that scenario to analyze the question of whether or not the identity of the ship changes through time (the "Growing Argument")? Depending on your own personal intuitions, answers to this question are going to vary, but that is how a thought experiment works. Again, like Thales' hypothesis of the earth floating on water as a ship floats on water, this example of an ancient thought experiment is very different from contemporary scientific experiments. However, these ancient examples do demonstrate to us that the ancients were thinking about (or trying to think about) some scientific ideas. That is good to know. Perhaps there has been some continuity in the history of human thought in that human beings have often wanted to adjudicate knowledges and beliefs using various types of scientific methods and philosophical approaches.

NOTES

1. Karl R. Popper, "Back to the Presocratics," in *Conjectures and Refutations: The Growth of Scientific Knowledge* (1963; repr., New York: Routledge, 2002), 200.

2. Grace Jantzen, *Power, Gender and Christian Mysticism* (New York: Cambridge University Press, 1995), 34–35.
3. Jantzen, *Power, Gender and Christian Mysticism*, 34.
4. J. H. S. Burleigh, ed. and trans., *Augustine: Earlier Writings* (London: Westminster John Knox Press, 1953), 26.
5. Ibid., 17.
6. Ibid., 27.
7. Popper, "Back to the Presocratics," 185.
8. Ibid., 187.
9. Ibid., 186.

Chapter Twelve

The Current Landscape

We have arrived at the end of our adventure. There isn't very much left to say. I have enjoyed being your leader in this adventure. I learned things about these topics and about myself as I wrote this book. Wherever you are, and whatever decade you are in, thank you for sharing this experience with all of us by reading this book. If you are reading this book in the 22nd century, I say hello! If the landscape of human knowledges and beliefs has changed at all by then, you will probably be reading this book to see what we thought about human knowledges and beliefs in the 20th and 21st centuries. My instincts tell me that probably not much will have changed by then. You will still be reading the works of philosophers of science Thomas Kuhn and Karl Popper, and, you know, I bet that by that time the theory of social construction presented by Peter Berger and Thomas Luckmann will have attracted an even greater following. The differences in the 22nd century will be the new scientific theories that are uncovered and the new engineering designs that are made. The ideas of religion, I suspect, will still be going strong. People will still be debating about what is the most "correct" truth about the world.

The current landscape of science and religion and knowledge and belief communities includes a few additional points. For one, although science is often understood to be in conflict with religion, it may actually be the world view of *scientism* that is in conflict with religion. Within the world view of scientism, everything in the world is viewed through the "lens" of science. Of all the activities in life, it is only the activity of science that is thought to have a meaningful role to play. With scientism, science really is placed in a privileged position over anything else, but not just privileged: within the world view of scientism, science becomes arrogant. Also, within a world view of scientism, you might be told that scientific activity is the *only* pathway to arrive at any kind of useful knowledge. In other words, religious activity is useless. Or, in a world view of scientism, you might be told that any meaning in human life is valuable only when meaning is based on scientific thinking. Leaving scientism aside, another way to look at the conflict between science and religion is to say that what is actually happening is that science is in conflict with some *forms* of *religion*—forms of religion that are based on absolute truths. We can certainly frame the question of "science and religion" in various ways, such that the conflict is about a struggle for religion in the face of science or the conflict is about a struggle for science in the face of religion. At any rate, as we have learned, a good scientist or engineer will tell you that science is not about truths, but science is about theories. Theories that can be very good, and provide us with a lot of useful and important knowledge, but theories, like faith, are prone to doubt.

There are times when we need to have doubts. Doubting is a normal part of human life and doubting influences both scientific and religious exercises. We might not always feel that doubting is a good thing, but doubting is a normal thing. I think that a fair religious person—a religious person who has really considered all the options for understanding knowledges and beliefs—would have to tell you that religion is not about truths. Religion is about a way of life. Religious thinking (religiosity) provides a way of life by suggesting ethical principles through which we can live—principles that ideally are not rigid and stiff, but principles that exist to guide us; to show us a *way* to live. Finally, the action of faith in our lives is important (whether or not we believe that a god exists). The action of faith in our lives keeps us asking questions, preventing our lives from becoming too stagnant. There is never a wrong time to be asking questions about knowledges and beliefs. An adjudicator asks questions just as much as an adjudicator makes decisions. In fact, the job of asking questions may even be more important than the job of making decisions. You can also make a decision about the acceptability of a knowledge or belief claim and then later on change your mind and make a different decision. Don't be discouraged if yesterday you thought one thing and today you think something else. All of us are like that. (Anyone who says they aren't like that is lying.)

During our adventure, we discussed justified beliefs and non-justified beliefs. Although it is the case that we have to be very careful in our scientific and engineering work to separate justified beliefs from non-justified beliefs (a humanitarian outlook depends on it), it is also alright if we use both justified beliefs (science) *and* non-justified beliefs (religion) to provide us with meaning and purpose in our own personal lives. Another philosopher of science, Paul Feyerabend (b. 1924, d. 1994), who learned from Karl Popper, explains in his book *Against Method* (first published 1975) that with knowledges and beliefs a variety of opinions is always best.[1] Feyerabend was referring to the fact that there are so many different domains of reality and truth out there in the world—multiple realities and multiple truths—an idea that all of us are now familiar with. Feyerabend was disliked by practicing scientists, because he was basically saying there isn't just one *type* of science available to us when we collect knowledge of states of affairs in the world. Indeed, the real life work of scientists has never really fit in well with the work of philosophers of science. Nor have the real lives of religious people fit in well with the work of philosophers of religion. That is just how it is. Philosophers of science and philosophers of religion, if doing their work properly, are functioning as neutral, dispassionate, and unbiased observers who work from the "outside" of science and the "outside" of religion. They evaluate the merits of science and religion in that way. Other folks who are functioning "inside" of science and "inside" of religion are going to have very different stories to tell about how these particular activities impact the world. That is just something to be aware of—the last thing I want to do is to give you the impression that the approach I have taken in writing this book was the only possible approach to take. In any non-fiction book, there is never just one possible approach, but many.

When writing a book an author chooses an approach that he or she feels is best. My intention in setting up this book in the form of an "adventure" was so that each of you could decide for yourselves how *you* would like to adjudicate the acceptability of human knowledges and beliefs. At times you may not have always agreed with my particular approach, but even still I hope you learned a lot from the philosophical and theological tools I presented to you. You can now take those tools and use them in your own lives, following whatever approaches you feel are best for understanding science and religion or knowledges and beliefs. It is commonplace at the end of any adventure, trip, or milestone, to feel a sense of satisfaction and also a sense of relief! You have finished the adventure. Congratulations! If I was with you right now, I'd give you a certificate which shows that you completed *Adventure in Human Knowledges and Belief*s. Since I am not with you (and may never meet you) I simply wish you well. Thank you for having enough trust in me to read through this book to the very end. As a writer, that means a lot. (Oh, and don't forget to read the Epilogue!)

NOTE

1. Paul Feyerabend, *Against Method*, 4th ed. (London: Verso, 2010), 25.

Epilogue: What Then Is *Reality*?

In life we see what we choose to see. Most of reality is hidden from us and the intricate workings of the world are scarcely visible to our poor eyes. Religions tell stories about light out of darkness, order out of chaos, and sight out of blindness. The greatest challenge in life is to move out of this state of confusion and into a realm of understanding. This is the great purpose of learning: to provide our human race with a means of moving forward, looking to our survival, as we search for the possibility of knowing reality as reality is. Is that where the truth is? How far away is the truth? Is the truth a mere delusion? We'll probably never know. We also aren't the first people to ask these questions which are as old as the world itself.

In one religious story the prophet Moses, a figure central to the Abrahamic religions (Islam, Judaism and Christianity), asks to "see" God but learns that no human being can "see" God and live. Is the reality of God so concealed that to know reality would mean death (i.e. darkness) or is this some unusual story from the ancient Near East that has survived centuries of oral transmission? Might it be that to see God, to experience reality, and to know the truth, is really to love our friends who are like us and to love the people who are not like us? Might it be that to know the truth is to have a pure heart, seeing life through a "lens" which allows us to see life as life is seen through the eyes of a child?

The ancient King Solomon of Israel, the teacher Jesus who travelled through the backwoods of Palestine, and the Prophet Mohammed (peace be upon him), all spoke about truth. The way we search for the truth is of no significance—whether we are Atheist, Theist, Agnostic, or Igtheist—unless we are first true about the things we know and the things we believe. Let us go into the world to find that kind of truth. For we know that if we keep searching for the truth we allow ourselves to escape the boundaries of human knowledge; we allow our human imaginations to soar.

I wonder how far we can go this time?

Glossary of Strange Sounding Words

(in the order as they appear)

Epistemology. The *form of knowledge*; a branch of philosophy and theology that asks questions about knowledge claims: What kinds of knowledge claims are legitimate and what kinds are not? How do we adjudicate the acceptability of a knowledge claim?

World view. The "lens" through which you see the world—your own personal opinion on any issue, the language you speak, the job you have, or the things you do for fun on the weekend. Any of these factors might contribute to your world view. Your world view also includes your knowledges and beliefs.

Adjudicator. A person who has to choose a single option from many options; a judge; a decision maker.

Knowledge claim. A statement of knowledge—scientific or religious—that a person makes.

Philosopher. A person who wonders about life, knowledge, eternity, morals, etc.

Legitimate. Right, correct, valid.

Abstract. Something that exists in a person's mind as an idea (rather than having a physical existence).

Framework. The structure of a system or idea; the rules of a system or idea.

Rational. A way of life; an attitude of being open to modification of one's world view; an attitude of accepting that all knowledge is corrigible, which means that all knowledge has the potential to be corrected or tweaked.

Justified. Describes something as having a good or valid reason for being the case.

Average. The sum of numerical values in a set of data divided by the number of values in the set of data.

Standard deviation. The degree by which values in a set of data differ from the average value of the data.

Empirical. A method of the natural sciences and engineering whereby we must experience or observe something in the physical world if we want to say that something is a description of reality or that something is a model for reality. For example, we read the mass of an object on a scale, we assess the acidity of a solution using a chemical test, or we read the temperature off a thermometer (compare with *Trans-empirical*).

Trans-empirical. Describes a world that is "outside" of human experience or beyond the visible world (see also *Transcendence* and compare with *Empirical*).

Transcendence. A situation that is "across" (beyond) the visible world (see also *Trans-empirical*).

Finite. Capable of being measured; limited in size (in contrast to *infinite* which means incapable of being measured and unlimited in size).

Social construction. The social world of a community was created by the community. The community members do not realize this. They believe their social world is something other than their own creation. Nevertheless the social world was in fact created by the community.

Social world. How we interact with each other in a community—how we understand our place in relation to the rest of the world and to everyone else around us; how we understand "reality."

Circular argument. An argument where an assumption is made and then the very assumption that was made is argued as "true" using the same assumption as evidence.

Supra-. A prefix meaning *above* or *superior*.

Theologian. A person who wonders about God, Allah, gods, goddesses, or any other superhuman agent.

Humanitarian. Promoting what is best for human beings and humanity; having the greatest good of human beings in mind.

Neanderthals. Primitive humans of the genus *Homo* and the species *neanderthalensis*. They lived about 200,000 to 30,000 years ago in what is now present-day Europe and Western Asia.

Scientism. A world view where everything in the world is viewed through the "lens" of science. Of all the activities in life, it is only the activity of science that is thought to have a meaningful role to play. Perhaps it is actually *scientism* and *religion* that are in conflict rather than science and religion being in conflict.

Bibliography of Works Cited

Barbour, Ian. *Religion and Science: Historical and Contemporary Issues*. New York: HarperCollins, 1997.
Berger, Peter L. *The Sacred Canopy: Elements of a Sociological Theory of Religion*. New York: Anchor Books, 1967.
Berger, Peter L. and Anton C. Zijderveld. *In Praise of Doubt: How to Have Convictions Without Becoming a Fanatic*. New York: HarperCollins, 2009.
Berger, Peter L. and Thomas Luckmann. *The Social Construction of Reality*. New York: Anchor Books, 1966.
Boyer, Pascal. *Religion Explained: The Evolutionary Origins of Religious Thought*. New York: Basic Books, 2001.
Burleigh, J. H. S., ed. and trans. *Augustine: Earlier Writings*. London: Westminster John Knox Press, 1953.
Einstein, Albert. *The World As I See It*. New York: Kensington Publishing Corp., 1984.
Feyerabend, Paul. *Against Method*. 4th ed. London: Verso, 2010.
Frankfort, H. A. and Henri Frankfort. "Myth and Reality." In *The Intellectual Adventure of Ancient Man: An Essay on Speculative Thought in the Ancient Near East*, 3–27. Chicago: The University of Chicago Press, 1946.
Huxley, Aldous. *Antic Hay*. 1923. Reprint, London: Vintage, 2004.
———. *The Doors of Perception*. New York: HarperCollins, 1954.
Jantzen, Grace. *Power, Gender and Christian Mysticism*. New York: Cambridge University Press, 1995.
Krauss, Lawrence M. *A Universe from Nothing: Why There Is Something Rather Than Nothing*. New York: Free Press, 2012.
Kuhn, Thomas S. *The Structure of Scientific Revolutions*. 4th ed. Chicago: The University of Chicago Press, 2012.
Küng, Hans. *Theology for the Third Millennium*. Translated by Peter Heinegg. New York: Doubleday, 1988.
Kurtz, Paul. *The New Skepticism: Inquiry and Reliable Knowledge*. Buffalo: Prometheus Books, 1992.
Luscombe, Philip. *Groundwork of Science and Religion*. Peterborough: Epworth Press, 2000.
Masood, Ehsan. *Science and Islam: A History*. London: Icon Books Ltd, 2009.
McCauley, Robert N. *Why Religion Is Natural and Science Is Not*. New York: Oxford University Press, Inc., 2011.
Mithen, Steven. *The Prehistory of the Mind: The Cognitive Origins of Art, Religion and Science*. London: Thames and Hudson Ltd, 1996.

Polanyi, Michael. *Personal Knowledge: Towards a Post-Critical Philosophy*. 1962. Reprint, Chicago: The University of Chicago Press, 1974.

Popper, Karl R. "Back to the Presocratics." In *Conjectures and Refutations: The Growth of Scientific Knowledge*, 183–223. 1963. Reprint, New York: Routledge, 2002.

———. *Conjectures and Refutations: The Growth of Scientific Knowledge*. 1963. Reprint, New York: Routledge, 2002.

———. *The Logic of Scientific Discovery*. 1959. Reprint, New York: Routledge, 2002.

Russell, Bertrand. *Why I Am Not a Christian.* New York: Simon and Schuster, 1957.

Seow, Choon-Leong. *A Grammar for Biblical Hebrew*. Nashville: Abingdon Press, 1995.

Smart, Ninian. *Worldviews: Crosscultural Exploration of Human Beliefs*. Upper Saddle River: Prentice-Hall, Inc., 2000.

Weinberger, David. *Too Big to Know: Rethinking Knowledge Now That the Facts Aren't the Facts, Experts Are Everywhere, and the Smartest Person in the Room Is the Room*. New York: Basic Books, 2011.

Wiebe, Donald. "Science and Religion: Is Compatibility Possible?" In *Beyond Legitimation: Essays on the Problem of Religious Knowledge*, 57–73. New York: St. Martin's Press, Inc., 1994.

———. "The Ambiguous Revolution: Kant on the Nature of Faith." In *Beyond Legitimation: Essays on the Problem of Religious Knowledge*, 162–176. New York: St. Martin's Press, Inc., 1994.

———. *The Irony of Theology and the Nature of Religious Thought*. Montreal: McGill-Queen's University Press, 1991.

Woodward, Andrew Ralls. "Biocompatible Hydrogels of Methacrylated Glycol Chitosan: A Focus on Improving Their Flexibility and Degradation Using Star-poly(trimethylene carbonate-co-D,L-lactide) triacrylate." Bachelor's thesis, Queen's University, 2010.

Index

adjudicator, 3, 7, 19, 22, 26, 28, 37, 48, 51, 56, 70, 73, 76, 77, 81, 83, 88
agnostic, 47–48, 57, 76
atheist, 46–48, 57, 76, 78
atom, 7, 10, 26, 49–50
Augustine, 84

Barbour, Ian, 58
belief, vii, 3–5, 20, 25, 34, 37, 46, 48, 54, 56, 65, 68; community, 33, 55, 56, 58, 78; justified, 16–17, 28, 74, 78; non-justified, 16–17, 74, 78
Berger, Peter, 33–34, 52, 55–56, 74, 77, 78–79, 87
Boyer, Pascal, 67, 68

cause. *See* explanatory force
circular argument, 52, 55
classical realist, 8–9, 65, 76
cognitive science, 37, 38, 39, 66
critical realist, 8–9, 76, 78

Darwin, Charles, 74

Einstein, Albert, 8, 63
electron, 7, 49
empirical, 18, 19, 27
engineering, 5–6, 8, 15
epistemology. *See* knowledge
explanatory force, 66, 69–70, 76

faith, 18, 28, 37, 39, 45–46, 48, 57, 77, 88
Feyerabend, Paul, 88
fides, 26
fiducia, 26

Higgs boson, 51
Hiphil verbal stem, 48
Homo sapiens, 3, 39
Huxley, Aldous, 11, 63
Huxley, Thomas, 45, 47
hypothesis, 69, 83

igtheist, 47–48, 57, 76
instrumentalist, 8–9, 65, 76, 78

Jantzen, Grace, 16, 82
Jesus, 91

knowledge, vii, 3, 5, 12, 15, 21, 37, 41, 45, 50; bar, 73, 74–75, 77, 78–79; claim, 7, 20, 26, 54, 67, 73–75, 77, 78; community, 33, 55–56; religious, vii, 5, 19–21, 35, 59, 66, 75–76, 82; scientific, 5–7, 11, 19–21, 34, 40, 49, 69, 75, 82
Kuhn, Thomas S., 6–7, 12, 15, 53, 54, 65, 74, 77, 78, 87
Küng, Hans, 58
Kurtz, Paul, 47

Lévy-Bruhl, Lucien, 42

97

Luckmann, Thomas, 33, 52, 55–56, 74, 77, 78–79, 87

McCauley, Robert N., 37, 40
Mithen, Steven, 40
Mohammed, 91
mythological, 35, 41–42

Neanderthals, 82
Newton, Isaac, 6, 53–54

Ottoman Empire, 50

paradigm, 7–8, 12, 53–55, 65
philosopher, 6; of religion, 35, 89; of science, 37, 89
Plato, 82–83
Polanyi, Michael, 9
Pope Pius XII, 51
Popper, Karl, 9, 15, 19, 74, 77, 78, 82, 87

rational, 15, 21, 34–35, 57, 70
rationality. *See* rational
religiosity, 38–39, 67
Russell, Bertrand, 68

scientific study of religion, 65, 66
scientism, 87

Smart, Ninian, 15
social construction, 33–34, 52, 55–56, 74, 77
Solomon, 91
speculative thought, 69

technology, 38, 40. *See also* engineering
Tertullian, 51
Thales, 82–83
theist, 46–48, 57, 76
theologian, 84; scientific-religious, 59, 74, 77
theory, 5, 8–9, 33, 55, 66; scientific, 8, 11, 19, 26, 53–54, 66, 78
thought experiment, 85
trans-empirical, 18–20, 27, 34, 38, 48, 52
trust, 26–27
truth, 8, 11–12, 35, 49, 59, 64–65; religious, 66

Weinberger, David, 74
Whewell, William, 6
Wiebe, Donald, 18–19, 26, 35, 45, 51, 58
Wilberforce, Samuel, 45
world view, 3, 15, 20–21, 34, 41, 54–57, 70, 77, 87

Zijderveld, Anton, 34

www.ingramcontent.com/pod-product-compliance
Lightning Source LLC
Chambersburg PA
CBHW070645300426
44111CB00013B/2267